ASPECTS of MODELLING

Track Layouts

Anthony New

Ian Allan
PUBLISHING

Dedication:
To Cyril J. Freezer, without whom this book would
not have been possible (or, perhaps, necessary!)

First published 2008

ISBN 978 0 7110 3355 9

Published by Ian Allan Publishing

an imprint of Ian Allan Publishing Ltd, Hersham, Surrey KT12 4RG.
Printed by Ian Allan Printing Ltd, Hersham, Surrey KT12 4RG.

Code: 0811/C

Visit the Ian Allan Publishing web site at: www.ianallanpublishing.com

Contents

Introduction

Like many modellers of a certain age, I grew up with the layout designs of C. J. Freezer, both in his 'Plan of the Month' for the *Railway Modeller* magazine and in his many books on layout design. I've always been a great fan of his and over the years have had huge amounts of pleasure studying his plans to see the clever ways he fitted everything in. Considering that some of his books were written four decades ago, the fact they are still in print suggests they continue to be valued as a useful source of ideas by modellers.

But in the decades that have passed things have changed greatly in the world of railway modelling, and many modellers now find his layout designs old-fashioned and unrealistic. What I used to think of as the more extreme end of finescale modelling has not only flourished but become mainstream, and the mass-production manufacturers like Bachmann and Hornby are now making models with detailing and accuracy that transcend almost anything seen on a finescale layout in 4mm scale, if you can forgive the track gauge compromise of '00' scale models.

Every railway modeller now wants a model railway layout that is realistic and not simply a glorified train set. A generation of younger modellers have grown up with finescale modelling as their aim and their expectation, and an older generation of modellers who (like me) played with a basic train set as a child have also returned to the hobby and want both to re-create the fun they had as children and to achieve something more worthwhile as well. They and I are faced with the same problem: What kind of model railway layout can we build? What kind of layout should we build? And how do we want to operate it?

There are so many questions to be asked, and every answer seems to bring forth more questions. Should we be building a model of a real location, or should we fake it? Can we even fit a real station into our spare room or attic without it looking silly? How did the real railway operate, and why did it persist in such weird track formations? Can we simply copy a real track plan, or do we have to change it? And if so, how? Do we need a fiddle-yard and if so, what sort should we be using?

All these questions and more will be answered in this book, and illustrated with a wide range of station plans taken from the real steam-age railway and adapted with more or less fidelity to the prototype. Many of the plans are explained in context, and where they deviate from the prototype this is usually indicated.

The plans I have drawn are designed to be as faithful to the prototype as is practicable in a reasonable space but also to be operable with realism and enjoyment. Inevitably compromises have been necessary to fit them into the kind of real-world spaces we have available for our hobby, in spare rooms and corners of garages, but if you have a little more space then the plans can be opened out or expanded to suit. Alternatively you could just use them as a source of inspiration for your very own layout design. In either case, there is a list of useful reference books in the Bibliography which I have used for these plans and which are worth getting hold of to help the modelling process.

Anthony New
August 2008

Note: The track diagrams are drawn with each square representing 1sq ft for '00' gauge (16.5mm between the rails), instead of the more correct 18.83mm track gauge. The size at which these drawings have been reproduced means that they are not necessarily accurate to scale.

Those modelling in 'N' gauge can use each square to represent 6in; 9in for TT gauge and for those modelling 'O' gauge each square represents approximately 1ft 9in.

The Country Station

The GWR Region

The GWR country terminus has been a deservedly popular inspiration for models for a very long time. A few years ago it seemed almost as if every railway modeller had to build a GWR branch terminus at some point in his modelling career, almost as a rite of passage. At exhibitions this did get rather boring for the viewing public. 'Oh, no! not another one!' seasoned modellers were sometimes heard to exclaim.

But as so often is the case, there were (and still are) excellent reasons for this. Firstly, if we consider the layout as an apprentice piece where the modeller can show off his acquired skills in the required form, the country terminus makes a good deal of sense. A believable model of a country station – particularly a GWR one which is well known to the onlookers – is an excellent choice for the developing modeller. It is compact, limited in size and scope, and easily carried to an exhibition. If space is limited in the home it can be set up quite easily and stored when out of use.

If it is a terminus it can be operated virtually on its own with just a small non-scenic fiddle-yard, and if it is modelled on one of the pretty GWR termini the task is both pleasing and enjoyable. In purely practical terms the country terminus takes some beating for a compact home layout that has the capability to be folded up and taken to the occasional exhibition.

But why, specifically, the GWR?

Again, there are reasons. The GWR had at least a dozen small termini, some of which are ideal for small spaces (though a few aren't!) and many of them were set in idyllic country scenery. In comparison the Midland Railway had comparatively few country termini; most cross-country branch lines sought to make junctions or end-on connections with other lines, and any town worth running to usually ended up with so much traffic the station grew quickly past the size expected for a compact layout or (as often) ceased to be a country station at all. Moreover, much of the land was industrialised and lacked the 'picture-postcard' appeal of the country station, though stations over the LMS and LNER can still be modelled.

Moreover as the GWR is so well known and well covered in reference books, the task of research is rewarding without being a lifetime's work. The excellent books by Karau and Potts (see Bibliography at the end of this book) are a good start here. Paul Karau's two volumes on GWR termini contain architectural drawings and photographs for the scratch-builder looking to make a highly realistic model. But for the modeller who wants to use either card kits or ready-to-use buildings such as Hornby's Scaledale, R. H. Clark's four-volume series *An Historical Survey of Selected GW Stations* is probably more useful as a source of ideas.

Take Faringdon, for example, which was the country terminus of the three-mile branch from the main line at Uffington. As you can see from plan 1.1, this station

Plan 1.1

Faringdon

GS Ground signal
ES Engine Shed
CP Cattle Pens
SB Station Building
FY Fiddle Yard
GF Ground frame
WT Water Tank
LD Loading Dock
    (coal for gas works)
LT Loading Gauge

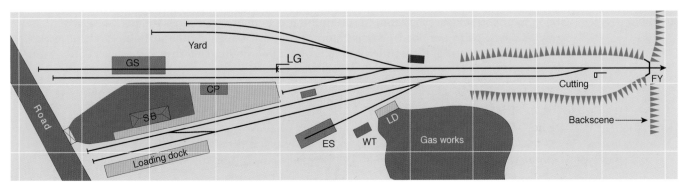

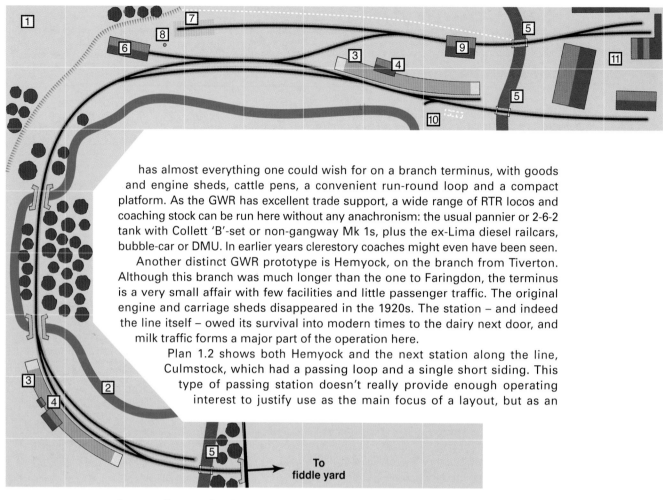

has almost everything one could wish for on a branch terminus, with goods and engine sheds, cattle pens, a convenient run-round loop and a compact platform. As the GWR has excellent trade support, a wide range of RTR locos and coaching stock can be run here without any anachronism: the usual pannier or 2-6-2 tank with Collett 'B'-set or non-gangway Mk 1s, plus the ex-Lima diesel railcars, bubble-car or DMU. In earlier years clerestory coaches might even have been seen.

Another distinct GWR prototype is Hemyock, on the branch from Tiverton. Although this branch was much longer than the one to Faringdon, the terminus is a very small affair with few facilities and little passenger traffic. The original engine and carriage sheds disappeared in the 1920s. The station – and indeed the line itself – owed its survival into modern times to the dairy next door, and milk traffic forms a major part of the operation here.

Plan 1.2 shows both Hemyock and the next station along the line, Culmstock, which had a passing loop and a single short siding. This type of passing station doesn't really provide enough operating interest to justify use as the main focus of a layout, but as an

To
fiddle yard

Plan 1.2

Hemyock &
Culmstock

1   Fields
2   River Culme
3   Platform
4   Station building
5   Level crossing
6   Engine shed
    (disused)
7   Carriage shed
    (demolished)
8   Water tower
9   Goods shed
10 Cattle pen
11 Dairy

intermediate station it gives just the kind of ambience that the real country lines had, with its level crossing that would be laboriously opened by hand to let the trains through. Interestingly enough the next station along the line, Uffculme, was almost identical, even to the river running past.

The GWR has always been a useful source of inspiration for minimum-space layouts and so here are two plans designed for narrow shelves, along one wall of a bedroom or garage. Both plans are a bare twelve inches wide, though as always another inch or two in width would be useful!

The first of these shelf layouts is Blagdon, plan 1.3, on a small branch line off the branch from Yatton to Congresbury. This station is simple enough to suit a first layout but the facilities are sparse and operation will be, I'm afraid, quite dull unless the layout is viewed primarily as a diorama or display. In the same space I would much prefer to model Blenheim & Woodstock, plan 1.4, which sounds like a Sixties pop concert but was in reality a branch from the GWR main line at Kidlington. This station is altogether busier and provides plenty of shunting opportunities, plus room to run round much longer passenger trains, such as day trips to the nearby stately homes. Both of these layouts need a small fiddle-yard and the cassette type is probably a good choice to allow a change of stock without manhandling delicate items.

Plan 1.3

Blagdon

1   Ground frame
2   Stables
3   Station building
4   Platform
5   Cattle dock
6   Gate
7   Road

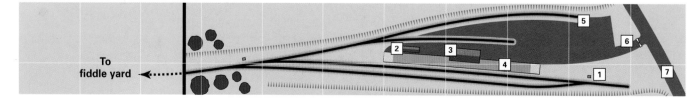

To
fiddle yard ◄┄┄┄

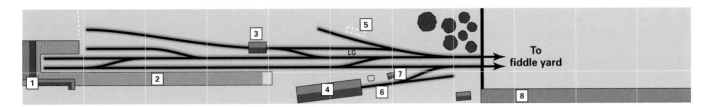

Other Regions

Although, as I said at the start of this chapter, there were good reasons to choose a GWR prototype for a compact model, time has moved on and it is no longer necessary to stick with the GWR. Books are available today on virtually every branch line in the country, so there is no excuse for maintaining the GWR fixation when one can so easily model the LMS, LSWR, SR, NER, GE, etc. Note that I have deliberately mixed up the Big Four post-grouping companies and some of the pre-grouping ones. Most of the lines and stations one is likely to be interested in will have been built long before the grouping period and will have been hardly altered during the Big Four era. Therefore one needs to research (say) a Great Eastern or North Eastern station rather than ask what an LMS or LNER station looks like, because to the latter question there is no answer.

But let us also look much further south at the Isle of Wight Railway. Holidaymakers from far afield will have both seen and probably travelled on this pretty and distinctive line when it was at its height of popularity in the 1950s and as the stations were all commendably compact, they make in some respects at least an ideal subject for the modeller who doesn't have much room for a layout or who wants to try his hand before committing time to a more complex layout.

The station at Bembridge (plan 1.5) was built by the Brading Harbour Improvement & Railway Company in 1874, taken over by the Isle of Wight Railway in 1898 and passed to the Southern Railway in 1923. It closed in 1953, but a few photos of it exist including the excellent aerial view in *The Aerofilms Book of Britain's Railways From the Air*. This provides enough detail for building construction including the Royal Spithead Hotel which backed onto the station and has since been demolished.

An obvious attraction of Bembridge shared by other stations on the Isle of Wight was its diminutive size – it has a single goods siding, a platform run-round, and even a small turntable instead of a headshunt to save space. Another iconic station on the line was Ventnor (plan 1.6), built by the Isle of Wight Railway in 1866 and accessed by the 1,312yd tunnel under St Boniface Down. The station was built on the site of a pre-existing quarry and various holes and tunnels in this were used as offices and stores by coal merchants, from a siding close to the cliffs.

Plan 1.4

**Blenheim &
Woodstock**

1   Station building
2   Platform
3   Goods shed
4   Engine shed
5   Cattle dock
6   Water tower
7   Signal cabin
8   Low relief
     houses
LG Loading gauge

Plan 1.5

**Bembridge,
Isle of Wight**

1   Half-timbered
     houses
2   Road
3   Allotmennts
4   Platform
5   Station building
6   Hotel
7   Turntable
8   Gate

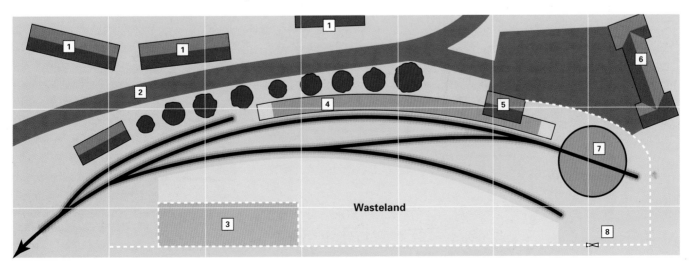

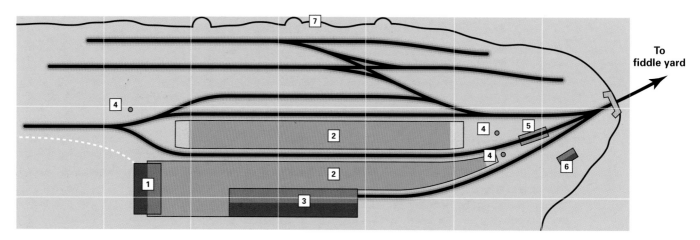

Plan 1.6

**Ventnor,
Isle of Wight**

1 Station building
2 Platform
3 Goods shed
4 Water column
5 Inspection pit
6 Signalbox
7 Chalk cliff with
   holes used for
   offices and
   stores

This station was also very compact for the number of platform faces and sidings it possessed and the chalk cliffs make an excellent scenic boundary for a model. The Subterranea Britannica website has many pictures of the station and is well worth checking out for other stations if you have internet access. Although these two stations have many virtues for the modeller, they do have a couple of major limitations which need to be appreciated. The first is the limited range of stock that the prototype saw in any given year. When the Southern took over the Island line, it brought over the 'O2' class 0-4-4 tank engines that became so strongly associated with the line. I don't think there is an RTR model of this class of locomotive but there are several kits available, as indeed there are for the older LSWR coaches used for many years before surplus London Underground carriages made their appearance.

The limited range of coaching stock that was used on lines like this may put off some modellers but is a major attraction to the modeller who likes to build rolling stock himself, from kits or drawings, and this will particularly suit those who don't like to limit themselves to scales and gauges with RTR support. Similar restrictions apply to many other branch lines that would otherwise make ideal models – for example the Lyme Regis branch which used Adams radial tanks for most of its life. The other limitation is in the variety of operation. The plain fact is that many branch lines saw only very basic and highly repetitive services, both for passenger and goods, and if you make much attempt to operate the station prototypically then you will suffer this problem too.

Of course you can cheat a little – don't we all! – but in some ways it is better to pick a station which saw more variety in real life and for which the track plan offers more interesting operation. Hawkhurst (plan 1.7), for example, had large coal pens and a sawmill adjacent, which will justify extra goods traffic.

Plan 1.7

Hawkhurst

1   Road
2   Coal pens
3   Station building
4   Platform
5   Cattle dock
6   Goods shed
7   Signalbox
8   Water tower
9   Coal stage
10 Crane
11 Oil tanks
12 sawmill
    (low relief)
13 Engine shed
14 Railway cottages

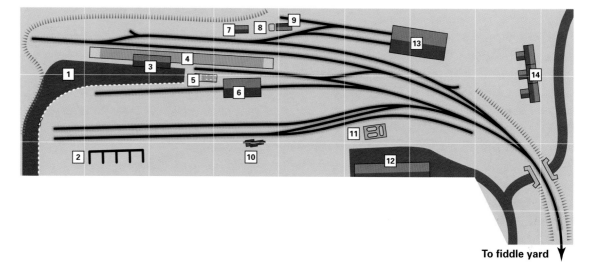

Hawkhurst had an interesting history before it passed into the South Eastern and thence to the SR. It was built for the fancily named 'Paddock Wood & Cranbrook Railway' by the famous (or infamous!) Colonel H. F. Stephens who built and ran so many light railways, usually on the proverbial shoestring and often with an astonishing array of weird and wonderful vehicles. The station building at Hawkhurst was built cheaply from corrugated iron, and as so often was the case, the line wound its way around the hillsides with only a half-hearted attempt to reach the towns and villages it nominally served. Hawkhurst's main claim to fame was as the terminus for hop-pickers' specials in season, and for schoolboys attending the nearby private school, who would have come direct from Charing Cross. Their luggage naturally formed a significant load for the local goods train, as did the pot plants from the local nursery destined for Woolworths. This kind of varied traffic always makes a fascinating addition to the usual vans and coal wagons, and if you can't find something equivalent at your chosen prototype station is well worth inventing to make life interesting.

It is common to think of country stations as being small, but that was often not the case. Land was usually cheap in the countryside and they often sprawled across it very inefficiently. So it is often necessary to compress even the smallest stations a little to get them into the space available and I do this almost as a formality to every plan I base on a prototype. One of the problems often found when fitting model termini into small spaces is providing enough length of run-round. Curiously enough the real station at Hawkhurst suffered from this too – the loco release spur was only long enough for tank engines and so, whenever main line engines worked the line, a separate engine had to be provided to shunt the train into a siding! This probably explains the double-track engine shed, though, as was so often the case, the shed fell out of use when rationalisation set in during the 'grouping' era of 1924-1947.

Many stations saw only short passenger and goods trains and relied on a simple run-round at the platform. Others placed the run-round further out away from the platform; this meant that after disgorging its passengers the local passenger train would be pushed back to the loop where the locomotive could run round it before setting back into the platform, a more involved manoeuvre than that usually seen on terminus layouts. The virtue of this arrangement was that the engine of a local passenger could leave the coaches in the platform and shunt the yard. Don't forget that many branch passenger trains would have odd vans that would need to be added or taken away from the formation.

CHAPTER

The Rest of the World

Termini

When one models a terminus one needs somewhere to send the trains off-stage, to represent the rest of the world. If you are lucky enough to have a large room or shed or garage available there are a great many possibilities for this which we will look at later in the book. However, it is likely that many modellers won't have this space available and will need something much more compact.

The traditional method of doing this is the so-called fiddle-yard of which there are a great many permutations. The simplest to build is undoubtedly a fan of sidings as in plan 2.1a, and in principle it is quite easy to use. If you are a finescale '00' modeller and build your own track you can still use shop-bought track here where nobody will see it except you. The two main snags with this are a certain amount of wasted space for the points, which is occasionally significant, and more importantly the problem of re-forming the train.

Although in the days of Tri-ang and Hornby Dublo models it was a simple matter to lift a locomotive or wagons off the track and replace them at the other end of the train, today's super-detailed models are easily damaged in handling and some other method is preferred. Obviously a run-round loop could be used as in plan 2.1b but this needs another two feet or so. It is better to put a spare locomotive on the other end of the train but this again takes up space and needs some shunting of locomotives (plan 2.1c). If tender engines are to be turned then a turntable will also be needed.

A method which has become very popular is the removable cartridge. Each cartridge is usually made from a piece of chipboard or wood with lengths of aluminium angle screwed to it, which act as sides to the carrier and also rails. Some kind of drawbolt is usually provided to lock the carrier into position, and electrical connections to the 'track' may be carried either through this or by wires with croc clips on. Many who use this technique also have a short secondary carrier which clips onto the far end for the locomotive.

When a train is run in, the carrier(s) may be unclipped and either slid along the fiddle-yard out of the way or lifted carefully onto a shelf, ready for another to be positioned. This method is perhaps the most compact arrangement and is one of

Plan 2.1

Fiddle yards for terminus

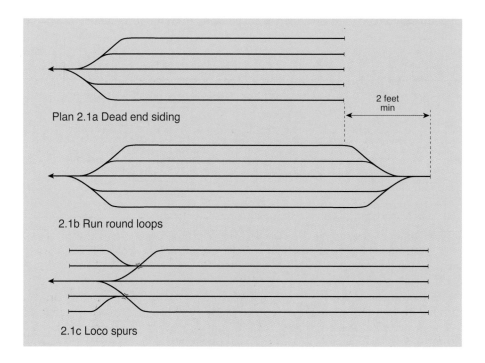

Plan 2.1a Dead end siding

2 feet min

2.1b Run round loops

2.1c Loco spurs

A simple fan of points on Bentley M.R. Group's 'Pengwynn Crossing'. This is very easy to build and use, but requires wagons and locos to be removed by hand. (Photo: Author)

the easiest to make. It also allows more storage in a given space than most others. Tender engines can easily be rotated by hand on their own short cassettes.

Where a branch railway line is modelled in a small space, fiddle-yards of any of these types are a convenient method of representing the rest of the world, and this is probably why so many exhibition layouts use them. But they are not without drawbacks. Firstly they require the operator to perform hideously unprototypical operations on a section of baseboard devoid of any scenery. At an exhibition this 'backstage' work is all well and good, in the name of artistic expression, but on a home layout where there is nobody watching, what is the point? Who is kidding whom?

Secondly, even on a small branch line, the amount of time spent working the yard is often as great as that spent on the main layout. At an exhibition, where a second operator is available, this can work well but usually does so only on branch lines with a very small amount of traffic. At home you will have to divide your time and energy between the two. The operator workload may also be too high to permit anything approaching main line train frequency, which is a big snag if one wants to model a station that did have a high train frequency. Both city stations and seaside termini would see a lot of trains at peak times, and many of these were compact enough to make nice models. So for these larger stations it may be better to avoid the traditional fiddle-yard.

One solution is to use a full-length turntable long enough to hold a complete train. Trains can arrive at and leave from the table until it is time to turn it through 180 degrees. This idea was popularised by the Rev. Peter Denny in his well-known (and completely fictitious!) 'Buckingham Great Central' layout and is very effective but will need some very good engineering to make it work reliably and pivot out of the way after use.

Through Stations

Despite the popularity of the terminus-to-fiddle-yard layout as the principal choice for a small layout, there were in reality far more through stations than termini. Familiarity with the GWR region has often blinded us to the fact that most branch lines elsewhere in the country didn't even have a terminus; they either joined another main line or met end-on with another company's branch which did. Many of the most interesting and/or scenic stations on branch lines were also through stations. The through station is of course a common choice for a continuous-run layout, and I will be looking at these in another chapter.

But here I want to consider the station as a prototype to model and operate in the same way that a branch terminus would be – in other words, prototypically and to a timetable.

I mention the word 'timetable' with some trepidation, because I know this is a term which divides modellers more than any other except perhaps the word 'finescale'. There are many modellers – myself included – who hardly ever run to a proper timetable and are happy to see realistic trains running in a representative but haphazard order around a layout, which we may euphemistically call 'watching the trains go by'.

But we see in Chapter 4 that to work at its best this really needs a main line where sufficient variety and intensity of trains exist to make the watching enjoyable. For the average country branch line this intensity and variety simply never occurred. Under these conditions, running trains to and fro may well get boring after a while, and this is why running to a timetable helps so much. The key point is that when one has devised and written down a timetable, one has created a set of requirements that will tax one's intellect and ensure the layout is operated prototypically. In other words, one is not simply playing trains but re-creating the operation of the real railway.

Much has been written about timetables in the past and I don't want to dwell too much on the topic in a book about layout planning, except to say that when done properly the timetable will not merely indicate the times that the local passenger train runs but will also have a means of selecting the goods wagons and vans which need to be carried between which stations on what occasions.

Once you have decided to operate a station prototypically in this fashion, it has certain consequences for the layout design. The obvious one is that you can't simply run trains around in circles even if the track plan permits this, as some do. You need to consider both ends of the visible layout as destinations to unseen but real and distinct places. An obvious way to do this is to use two fiddle-yards, one at each end of the station modelled as in plan 2.2a. This has a drawback in the length needed, though if you generally operate the layout at exhibitions this won't be a problem – you can set up the scenic sections in your home to check them out, perhaps with one or other fiddle-yard at a time, and only have both connected at the exhibition.

The cassette system in use on Tim Maddock's 'Bleakhouse Road' layout, showing both long and short cassettes. Note the small folded brass clips which align the cassette and transmit power. (Photo: Author)

If your layout is to be run at home as well as at exhibitions, you can use a short corner section to turn one of the fiddle-yards through a right angle (plan 2.2b). This can be taken further with additional straight sections used only at exhibitions (where the space is available) in place of the corner section used at home. In a domestic setting one will easily see how a pair of fiddle-yards can be fitted into odd spaces around the room and the tracks run to them along the walls, perhaps via lifting sections over doorways.

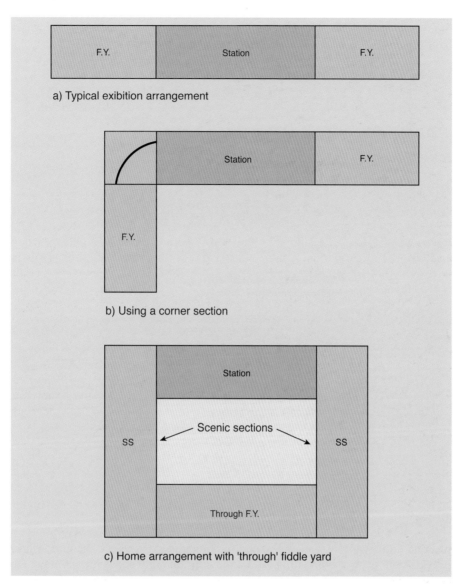

Plan 2.2

Fiddle yards for through stations

a) Typical exibition arrangement

b) Using a corner section

c) Home arrangement with 'through' fiddle yard

However, a more fundamental problem with through stations which is sometimes missed until the layout is built, is that as most trains pass straight through the station with only a brief stop, you have to spend about twice as much time operating the two fiddle-yards as you would on a terminus-to-fiddle-yard layout, and possibly less time operating the station itself. This can get to be a real drag unless you have a very streamlined method of operating the fiddle-yard.

There are various ways of dealing with this. One is to make sure you have a friend or two available for running sessions, particularly if you run the layout at exhibitions. Another is to pretend one of the lines has been closed and that the station operates as a terminus. You could even couple the through station to a terminus, and it doesn't have to be your own terminus – it is very easy to knock up a quick adapter board which interfaces between two different layouts. The centre section can be switched between the layouts each end so that trains don't stop or jerk as they cross the boundary.

I often wonder why more modellers don't do this at exhibitions in the UK. It is of course a step toward the modular layout that American modellers often use, where a standard baseboard width and track spacing is agreed so that boards made by different modellers can be joined for an operating session.

A good method of coping with a through station at home is to bend the lines around the walls of the room to meet a central storage section on the other side (plan 2.2c). This has several advantages, chief of which are the chance to use

Plan 2.3

**Fiddle yards for
through stations**

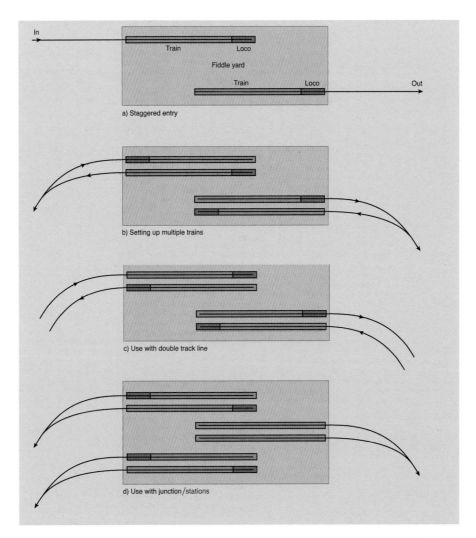

a) Staggered entry

b) Setting up multiple trains

c) Use with double track line

d) Use with junction/stations

just one fiddle-yard instead of two and to get some extra scenic sections. These provide both extra viewing time for the moving train and space for shunting. On many country stations, where traffic was sparse, the station could only be shunted properly using the main line each side.

With a single cassette-type fiddle-yard for a through station, provided the two entries to the fiddle-yard are staggered as in plan 2.3a, it is quite easy to place one cassette against each track and run a train around from one (filled) cassette to the other (empty) one via the through station. At this point the operator will need to return to the fiddle-yard and set up the next train, which is fine. But I much prefer to set up the next trains in both directions as in plan 2.3b, using either a single point or a small fan of points on each track as shown. This means one can delay the return to the fiddle-yard and can immerse oneself in the station operation a while longer. With more points and a well-rehearsed timetable, you can (in principle) set up several trains this way, though on a branch line the prototype's re-use of locomotive and rolling stock on successive services could make this problematic.

If the cross-country branch station is a double-track one, as quite a number actually were despite what you might think from wandering around model railway exhibitions, the scheme can be modified to suit (plan 2.3c).

Another option which can also work well is represented in plan 2.4. This uses storage loops and sidings instead of cassettes and the principal advantage here is speed. Much of the time a train can be reversed simply by running a new loco from one of the loco spurs onto the other end of the train, leaving the original train engine isolated when it moves out, until it too can be run to a loco spur.

The plan also shows a few through loops which deserve some comment. A continuous run is actually useful for running in locomotives as many do not deliver their best slow-speed performance unless run in for an hour or so, and although this can be done with the locomotive resting upside down on the worktop, it is usually better done on the track.

But one of the objections to having through loops like this is the temptation to run trains around as one would do in a basic train-set oval. Whether you succumb to this temptation depends on you! If you look on the locomotives as individuals then you won't want to run a passenger train around the circuit more than once, but will ensure the loco at least returns the way it came. In this case the loco should always be run round its train to reverse the journey. Or should it?

Consider a cross-country branch line such as Pencader (plan 2.5). Now I would not claim this station to be a 'typical' branch line station, since I picked it specifically because it was a good deal more complex than most stations on single-track branch lines. The sad fact is that most such stations were much too simple to provide much entertainment and most country stations with an interesting level of sidings were actually on double-track stretches!

But if we do pick such a station as this, which has significant traffic flow, then the majority of trains in each direction are likely to run further afield than the

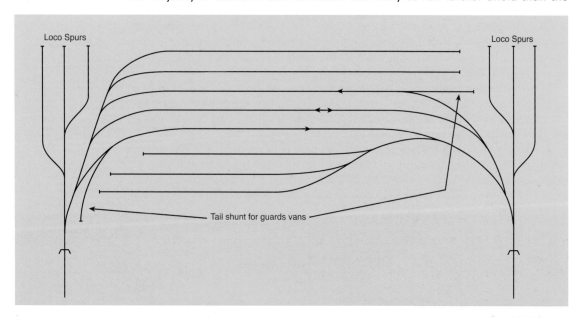

Plan 2.4

Storage Loops (through & dead-end) with loco spurs

Loco Spurs

Loco Spurs

Tail shunt for guards vans

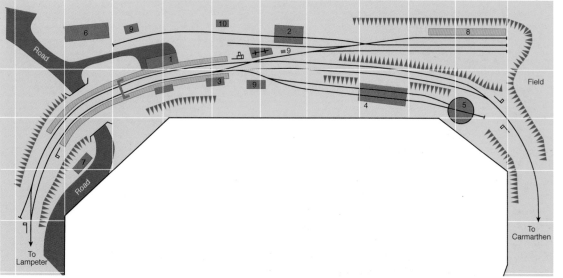

Plan 2.5

Pencader GWR

1 Station building
2 Goods shed
3 Signal cabin
4 Engine shed
5 Turntable
6 Sawmill
7 Smithy
8 Loading bank
9 Hut or shed
10 Weighbridge & office

Road

Road

Field

To Lampeter

To Carmarthen

branch itself, since the average branch line generates and receives only a very small amount of purely local traffic. When these services return they will do so with a different loco. These trains, particularly passenger trains, can be served easily with terminal roads as shown and a second loco is run onto the back of each train.

But most other non-passenger trains, such as minerals, coal, stone and the like, whether terminating on the branch or using it as a through route, will usually run empty in one direction and full in the other. In this case it is far easier to use the through loops for the distinct full and empty wagon flows, and just change the loco on the end. I suspect, however, that after a while the trains will begin to look familiar and it would be better to drop off the odd wagon or three for occasional journeys to add variety, and perhaps even to change the guard's van. The tailshunts I have shown on the loops in the fiddle-yard can be used for this purpose.

On the Pencader plan I have therefore curved the track around the walls of what I assume to be an 11ft room to suit a through-type fiddle-yard. If you have a lot more length available then curvature in the station can be eased or even avoided completely. I have also shown the engine shed, although this was removed along with the tiny 28ft turntable by 1930.

Goods trains are a slightly different problem. You would not expect individual wagons sent in one direction to return on the next train, or indeed in the same sequence much later, because they would wait at different stations for a different number of days. The easiest way to make sure of this is to remove the wagons from the track entirely. Another option is to use a card system or even a computer program which randomises the wagon loads and specifies the journeys to be done by each wagon on which dates.

If done properly this kind of load preparation can be a fascinating part of running a model railway because it mirrors the way real loads were carried on the railway. Remember, wagons weren't conveyed for fun – they carried paying loads or were returned empty for future paying journeys.

Of course you don't have to take so much care with wagon loads if you don't want to. After nationalisation in 1948 the old wooden-bodied open wagons disappeared quite quickly and steel-bodied wagons became more common. With these, one wagon looks very like another, and provided there is enough

A rotating table in use on Richard Dagger's unfinished layout 'Lower Hamworthy'. Note the way the tracks are splayed out at the ends for accurate alignment of each track in turn. The 'Denny' style turntable usually has the tracks parallel and uses points on the main baseboard to access them in turn. (Photo: Author)

variety in the trains, and the length is changed a little each time, then you don't have to be too dedicated about changing the running order.

Realism is best served by altering the train somehow, adding or swapping wagons, and by changing locomotives. If the locos you use are at all distinctive they ought to return on the next train, or at least a subsequent one. Similar arguments apply to obviously loaded or empty trains of china clay, iron ore, stone, or steel coil, all of which could be seen on various lines. Although it may be thought that these loads were essentially main line traffic, many of the starting and ending points for this traffic were actually on secondary lines, whether or not they were strictly referred to as branches.

The same is true for van and livestock traffic. Many country lines would see intensive cattle or sheep traffic on market day. Don't forget also that several lines near racecourses carried enormous quantities of race-related trains including horseboxes and passenger trains, run as specials. It is difficult to model one of these racecourses accurately because they often had an enormous number of sidings but one could always model one of the stations on the line that saw this traffic.

A rotating table built for the author's layout 'Charlotte Street.' In principle several tracks can be used simultaneously but aligning the tracks in construction is difficult. (Photo: Author)

Junction Stations

If you are intending to model a through station and are prepared to construct and operate the fiddle-yards to do so, then one way to increase the variety of operation is to model a junction station. It isn't difficult to run two lines into the same fiddle-yard, particularly if the cassette system is used as in plan 2.3d.

I had intended to give several examples of these to make my point, but on checking my books I found that decent-sized junctions stations on single-track branch lines were rather less common than I expected. In fact one of the few I found which is suitable is Congresbury, on the Cheddar Valley Line (plan 2.6). Congresbury was that rarest of delicacies, a junction of a branch line from another branch, in this case the lesser of the two branches being the Wrington Vale Light Railway, running to its terminus at Blagdon which we have already seen. The station has just enough sidings and facilities to provide fulfilling operation without being too large to model accurately, and the track plan is complex enough to look interesting without being unmanageable.

Plan 2.6
Congresbury

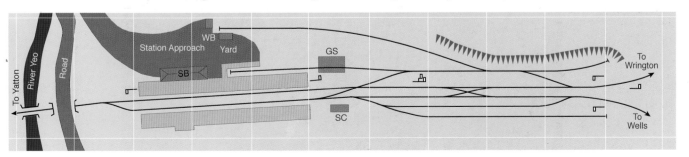

I looked at several other junction plans including both Yatton and Kemble before rejecting them. Yatton was actually a much bigger station than is often appreciated, with a veritable maze of pointwork that would be impossible to model with RTR points. And although one can certainly try and simplify it, that itself is very difficult to do without losing either the functionality or the appearance of the original. In fact, although this sounds strange, I found it far easier to simplify the huge stations at Leeds Central and Glasgow St Enoch than the country junction at Yatton.

Kemble is a much easier station to model accurately, and I have seen good exhibition models of it. But both junctions have a major problem for the modeller, which is that they sat on main lines which passed a great deal of fast heavy traffic. In my view, even if you can build a model of either station, it is very difficult to operate it realistically in the manner discussed in this chapter. It seems to me that the only chance of reproducing the main line traffic flows realistically is to turn the layout into a 'watching the trains go by' model instead, which makes it quite a different beast.

If you do want to model a junction station and to operate it with a fiddle-yard then a 'secondary' main line is desirable to reduce the train frequency. In this case, I think a large dose of invention is just as useful as research, and some freelance sketches on the back of the proverbial envelope may be the best way forward. If you are keen on pre-nationalisation modelling this could even be a station used jointly by different regions, which would allow trains of different companies to visit the station. This would still work in BR days since up to the end of steam most regions still operated much as they had done in grouping days.

Plan 2.7 shows some basic ideas for different types of junction. These are mostly taken from the GWR but similar variety was found in other regions. At Savernake (plan 2.7a) a double junction off the main line allows trains to run from main line to the branch and vice versa, with a small bay off the branch for auto-coaches and (latterly) DMUs. Both Yatton and Kemble on the GWR used similar arrangements. Brent (plan 2.7b) and Tiverton Junction (plan 2.7c) used another common layout in which the branch fed directly into a platform loop. Here passenger trains from the branches can leave in either direction on the

Hidden Storage Loops in use on the Stafford Railway Circle's modern image continuous-run layout 'Littleton Jctn.' (Photo: Author)

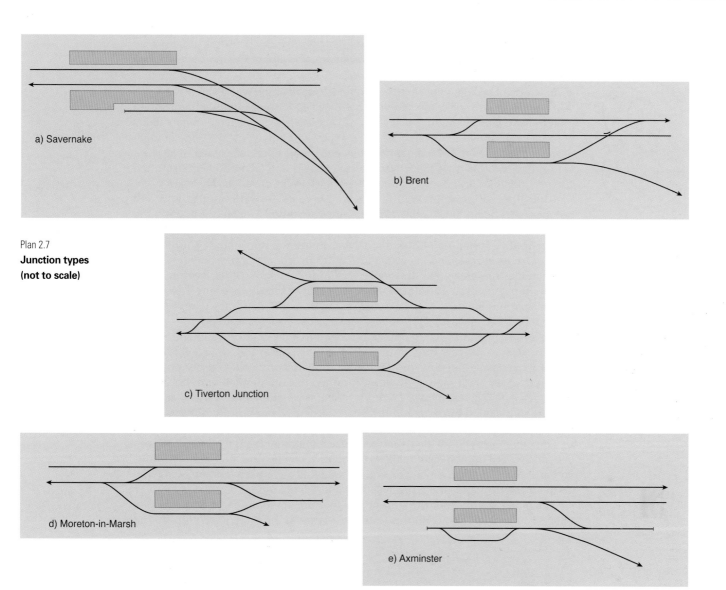

Plan 2.7

**Junction types
(not to scale)**

a) Savernake

b) Brent

c) Tiverton Junction

d) Moreton-in-Marsh

e) Axminster

main line using the crossover but this was not always the case; at Moreton-in-Marsh (plan 2.7d) the track planners have obviously gone out of their way to prevent this, perhaps due to a dislike of facing points. The most extreme example was probably Axminster (plan 2.7e) in which there is no direct access to the main line at all, except by reversing down a siding! (Those familiar with the station will know there was another more direct connection for goods trains but for a variety of reasons this was not always used.)

Obviously the style preferred depended on the ratio of through traffic on the branch to shuttle traffic. Many branches had a very basic passenger service which simply ran too and fro to connect (if you were lucky!) with those main line services that deigned to stop. Run-round loops were provided on branches that were likely to run passenger trains with several coaches, and single bays on lines that saw only push-pull fitted sets.

We'll be discussing goods traffic in more detail later but it should be appreciated that unless there was some particular industry that produced a large flow of specialised traffic (what we would now call trainload) then goods could be carried quite easily by the local stopping goods train. Since this would be expected to shunt at each station en route, the lack of a direct connection to the main line would be no problem. So when you are planning your junction station, it is worth spending some time thinking what sort of traffic you will run on it to make sure the layout will cope.

CHAPTER

To the Seaside!

One way of avoiding the limited operational scope of the typical country branch terminus is to select a prototype that received far more frequent and varied traffic, and in many ways the ideal station to choose is the seaside terminus. Many of these were compact or even cramped stations which don't need a huge amount of space to do them justice; most have obvious scenic boundaries, and most were very pretty too. Many of them also received main line locomotives during the summer months, plus occasional but intensive van traffic of various kinds.

After the war's end in 1945 it took a few years for rationing to end and prosperity to begin, but by the 1950s almost everybody fancied following the invitation of the poster-painters to head south 'Because Summer Comes Earlier in the South'. Idyllic paintings of St Ives, Penzance and Padstow drew our families to the seaside and the train journeys there (for cars were still rare before 1960) made the journey all the more thrilling. For many of us, seeing these posters today invokes nostalgic memories of day excursions to the seaside or annual summer holidays in the South West of England. For those who are keen to model British railways of the 1950s, the seaside terminus is ideal.

So let's start with a favourite holiday location, St Ives in Cornwall. The St Ives branch was – as its name implies – a branch line and unlike its larger contemporaries at Padstow and Penzance, St Ives hardly saw tender engines. For most of its life it managed with Churchward's small 4500 and 4575 class 2-6-2 tank locomotives. But the compact size of the station and its pretty scenery more than make up for this, and the sharp curves of the prototype are a great help in fitting the layout into a small room of only 8ft length (plan 3.1).

Operation is therefore a little limited but on the other hand it is possible even in a small room to produce a realistic model that can be operated prototypically, and as it is a real station in a well-known area it is quite easy (and enjoyable) to do the research necessary to produce and operate the model.

The small station was situated in a highly picturesque resort and changed little through GWR and BR times until 1961 when the engine shed closed. The

Plan 3.1

St Ives (GWR)

1   Down Home
2   Engine shed
3   House
4   Advance starter
    and engine shed
5   Viaduct
6   Sand
7   Starter
8   Platform
9   Goods shed
10 Station building
11 Fence
12 Retaining wall
13 Road
14 Low relief town
    houses

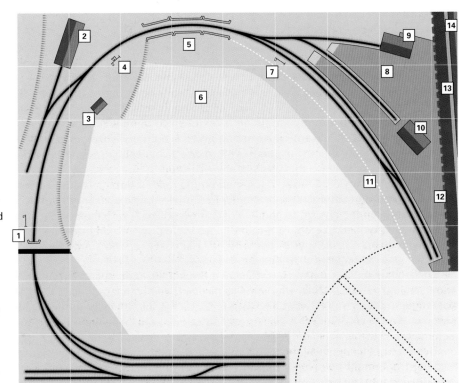

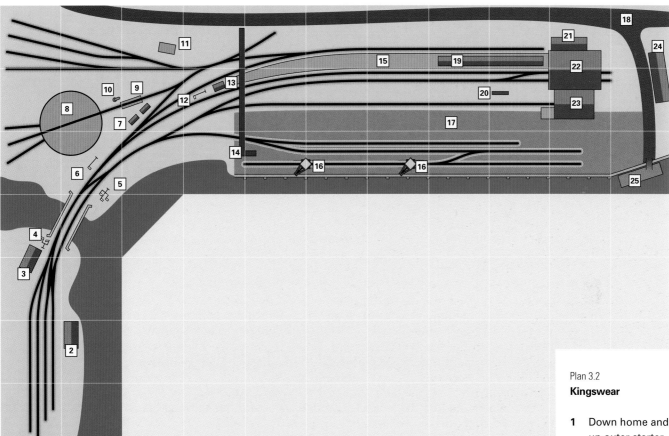

To fiddle yard

Plan 3.2

Kingswear

1 Down home and
  up outer starter
2 Boat house
3 Lime kilns
4 Down inner
  home
5 Up advance
  starter
6 Platform starter
7 Huts
8 Turntable
9 Inspection pit
10 Water column
11 Water tower
12 Platform 1
  starter
13 Signalbox
14 Footbridge
15 Platform
16 Electric cranes
17 Goods yard
18 Road
19 Platform awning
20 Ground frame
21 Station building
22 Train shed
23 Goods shed
24 Royal Dart Hotel
25 Pontoon landing
  stage (foot
  passengers)

goods shed and sidings closed in 1966 and in 1971 the station was demolished and rebuilt in its current minimalist form, but the surroundings remain today for a photographic expedition. The key to capturing St Ives is in the cliff-side scenery, and modelling both the drop to the sea and the town houses behind the station will be a worthwhile challenge.

Another favourite location in the South West which was rather busier than St Ives was Kingswear, in South Devon. This was one of the few main line termini to be single-track and yet it not only saw express steam locomotives in the 1950s but still does today! Plan 3.2 is my arrangement of this for the corner of a moderately large room, and the track plan is as nearly accurate as is practical for the period from about 1930 (when the re-modelling and extending of the platform was finished) to 1967 when the carriage sidings were removed. Although compressed in length, the platforms will hold six- or seven-coach trains. I have shown the footpath to the pontoon for the passenger ferry but not the slipway to the car ferry the other side of the hotel; this would take another foot or so to model fully and would be worthwhile if possible.

The carriage sidings are unusually short and hold only about three coaches each (a little less than the prototype) so a train has to be split in half to store it just as in the prototype, and the length of headshunt in the bay platform limits this as much as the siding length. The short loop on the bay platform line is not to run round trains but to allow access to the turntable when the bay platform is full. As you will appreciate, passenger trains tend to arrive at a seaside station in groups and the stock has to be kept somewhere until it needs to leave again. Stock would fill the sidings on summer Saturdays and some would be sent back to Paignton and beyond.

Depending on how busy the station was going to be that day, the driver of an arriving train might be given different instructions by the signalman; he might be signalled into the bay, and told to back the train out when the passengers had

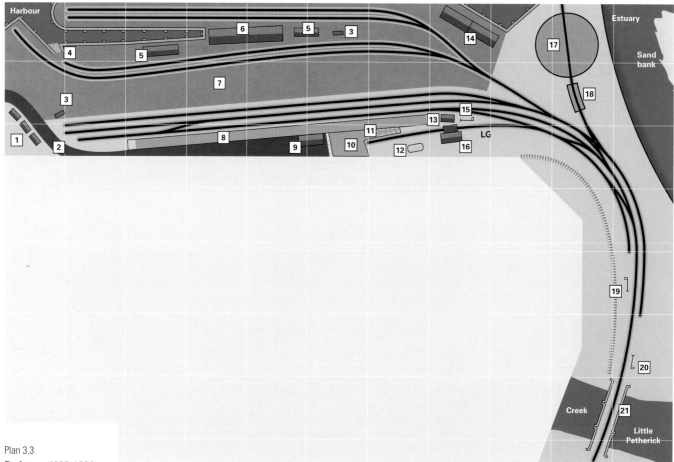

Plan 3.3

Padstow 1933-1966

1   Houses
2   Road
3   Old carriage
    body
4   Slip way
5   Offices
6   Fish processing
    shed
7   Yard
8   Platform
9   Station building
10 Loading dock
11 Cattle pens
12 Oil tank
13 Signalbox
14 Stores
15 Up starter signal
16 Goods shed
17 Turntable
18 Ash pit
19 Down home
    signal
20 Up advance
    starter
21 Girder Bridge
LG Loading gauge

disembarked, ready to split the train in two and push both halves back into the carriage sidings separately; he might be signalled into the main platform and told to run the locomotive round its train ready to leave immediately, or perhaps to shunt it back into the bay to make room for another arriving train.

He would probably want to run the engine into the turntable line to water it, to oil the motion, and (if it was a tender locomotive as usual) to turn it ready to leave. If the locomotive had completed a long journey and was due to go 'on shed' it would run light back to Newton Abbot, but if it had come on fairly recently or the station was busy he might hang around for a return journey.

One of the particular attractions of Kingswear was that, like Weymouth (see Chapter 8), it dealt with a lot of non-passenger traffic too. For many years it was a main coal importation dock for the local gas company and had cranes there for the purpose, though these are gone today.

The layout can be used with a fiddle-yard or a set of storage loops or some other arrangement. I have deliberately telescoped the main line to use the tunnel as a scenic break for the fiddle-yard but if preferred you could easily extend the layout around the room to model either more of the main line, or perhaps the next station at Churston. This is probably a good point to remind you that Kingswear, like other lines that are still open today, can be viewed online on Google maps (see bibliography); in fact if you follow the line to Churston you can (at the time of writing) see a steam train on the line!

I have tried to include signal locations on most plans in this chapter, though this is not generally practical in the whole book if only because many of the busier stations had far too many signals to be able to locate precisely on a small-scale model plan. However, if you are planning to model any of the stations in this chapter (or others) then it is worthwhile investing in the relevant reference book. The GWR and SR station plan books listed in the Bibliography have both scale track plans and signalbox diagrams which (together with photographs of the location) will answer many of the signalling questions.

Of course the GWR had no monopoly on the South West coast; the Southern dipped its 'withered' arm into Cornwall and one of the fingers rested on Padstow. Padstow never achieved quite the same level of popularity as its competitors but unlike many holiday resorts it did have a major traffic in fish, and this makes it an interesting choice for a model.

It is customary on models of seaside stations to place the sea at the front of the layout but for a change I have done the opposite in plan 3.3. One reason is that the south jetty extended a considerable distance into the harbour and any scale model – even a compressed one as here – would have difficulty in showing this to a believable length. So here it is pushed up against the backscene where its deficiency is (I hope) less annoying.

Of course the task of compressing real stations into a reasonable space is one of the challenges in presenting model plans. It is rarely possible to shrink everything in proportion and Padstow is a case in point, since the dock lines extended a long way from the station. I have chosen to shrink the sidings and platform lines to a length at which they are still usable, but as a result the dockside sidings and jetties have been shortened much more than the station itself. If you have more space you can correct this. However, apart from this essential compression, the rest of the station is pretty much as the real thing was from the 1930s when the fish dock was rebuilt, until it closed in 1966. The station was sparsely signalled but the distinctive ex-LSWR lattice signal post carrying the platform starter is worth modelling even if you don't normally bother with such things.

There is room to model a reasonable area of the estuary and sand bars in the corner, and even the well-known girder bridge over Little Petherick creek, though I admit to moving it a little closer to the station than it should be! As a small harbour that got most of its livelihood from fishing, there wasn't a great deal of non-fish goods traffic and the long siding next to the run-round was used mainly as a carriage siding. It is unfortunate that most published pictures of the station are taken from the same angle, but once again the station buildings and the ground itself remain for inspection even though the rails have departed. The old trackbed is now a cycle path, so close inspection of the Little Petherick bridge is now easier than ever.

Another favourite South-Coast destination was the busy but delightfully compact SR station at Swanage (plan 3.4). Unlike Padstow, the station at

Plan 3.4
Swanage

1   Stone yard
2   Up advance
    starter
3   Gate
4   Stream
5   Catch point
6   Engine shed
7   Turntable
8   Coal stage
9   Water tower
10 House
11 Up starter
12 Platform
13 Goods shed
14 Loading dock
15 Coal bins
16 station building
17 Signalbox
18 Yard
19 Down home
    bracket signal
LG Loading gauge

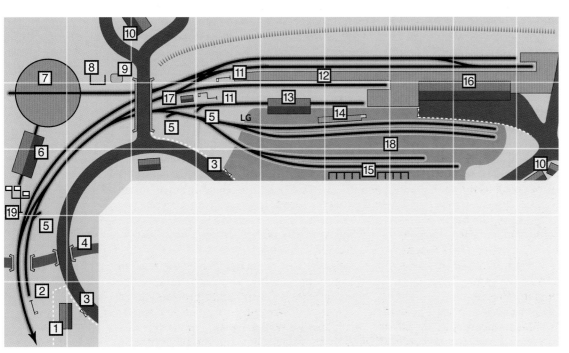

Swanage is very much still with us, courtesy of the Swanage Railway preservation group, and still features regular steam travel through the summer. The old goods yard is now a parking area for taxis and buses but the rest of the station and track is pretty much as it was in its heyday which is a great boon to the modeller. The unusual bent loco shed line is a nice feature and fits into a convenient corner much too well to refuse!

In its early years the station had considerable coal and stone traffic, but postwar it had only two goods trains a week and in summer the sidings were used primarily for coaching stock. The track plan and signalling are correct for the period between 1945 until the yard closed in 1967. The bracket down home signal is a splitter for the two platforms and carries a small shunting arm for the goods yard. As usual both platforms had their own starter signals but the goods yard would use the advance starter by the main line past the bridge. A train being formed at the station would be quite likely to overhang the yard entry points and this signal probably also acts as an outer home, that is, the normal limit of shunting.

One of the differences between freelance models and real stations is that station buildings and goods sheds in the latter often obstructed the view, rather than neatly sitting at the back of the layout, so in plan 3.4 I have naughtily moved the goods shed along a bit to avoid obscuring locos standing at the platform. You could easily reverse this if you prefer, or even model the layout from the other side. However, having the yard at the front helps enormously in shunting, especially if you use non-automatic couplings such as 3-link.

The plans so far will need to operate either as part of a larger layout or with a small fiddle-yard. As discussed in the last chapter, when you are operating a main line station with heavy traffic and a fiddle-yard all by yourself, the workload can be very high. One solution to this problem is to reduce the amount of fiddle-yard traffic to a minimum and the next few plans show various ways of doing this.

Ramsgate Harbour (plan 3.5) was built by the London, Chatham & Dover Railway in 1863 as an extension from its line to Margate but the station didn't survive long into grouping as the tunnel next to the station was steep and difficult to work. The SR built a cut-off to Dumpton Park in 1926 which forms the main line today, and closed the old terminus the same year, though I'm told the train shed survived until 1998.

In practical terms the tunnel and cliffs make an excellent place to hide a fiddle-yard, and if trains are habitually banked through the steep tunnel one might get away without too much awkward shunting in the fiddle-yard. The station was always very cramped (good for a model!) and the small turntable was no doubt fitted and kept for that reason just like the traverser at Birmingham Moor Street.

If building the layout myself I'd make some assumptions about what could have happened to it over time. If the station survived intact through the grouping period and was available in wartime for use with the docks, postwar expansion of commercial traffic at the docks might have made it economically viable through the Beaching period as happened at places like Weymouth. One could then justify extending the goods line into the adjacent docks to see trains of wagons arriving behind a Bo-Bo or Co-Co locomotive, though in all

Plan 3.5

Ramsgate Harbour

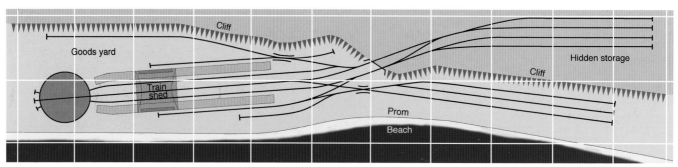

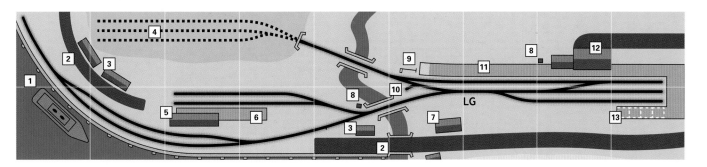

probability the turntable would have been removed by then. The main point of this variation on real life is to create a great deal of extra potential traffic for the station and in particular to provide for some shunting potential on the layout itself. This is, in my view, the key requirement of any home shelf layout as it ensures that driving trains through a hole in the scenic wall is not the only thing you end up doing!

Plan 3.6 takes this a stage further into an entirely fictional seaside scene which is clearly inspired by Weymouth but is quite different in design. Once again there is a main line connection to hidden loops which represent the 'rest of the world' but the main activity will be shunting of goods wagons and vans around the dockside. These can be operated from the front of the layout. Many docks like this lost their passenger services entirely by BR days but there is room for a DMU or auto-coach if you wish.

In practical terms the layout is arranged a bit like a three-legged stool. One leg is the hidden storage loops, another leg is the dockside, and the third is the in-view sidings. Goods trains arriving at the station would be shunted into the sidings to clear the station, and individual wagons would then be shunted as needed to either the goods shed, the cattle pens, a loading platform or the dockside itself.

As at Weymouth, when a large ship arrived with fresh produce there would be several trains of empty vans waiting to be filled, and these would be shunted urgently between sidings and dockside. When filled, they would be formed into trains (probably plural) and sent off immediately.

However, in less busy times a small ship might arrive before a train, perhaps with timber or general goods that would need to be stored in a warehouse for a while before vans arrived to take them on. Goods would also arrive for export and once again these might arrive some time before the ship was ready to take them onward.

In general terms it wasn't desirable to leave loaded wagons lying around. Not only did it tie up the railway company's vans unnecessarily, but the railway company considered that its part of the deal was finished when the goods had been transported to the destination. It didn't want any responsibility for pilfering or damage after this point, so it would be up to the merchant to see to storage until his ship was ready. At the larger ports transit sheds were usually provided for this but even a small harbour would usually have some warehouse space available.

So there is considerable scope for wagon and load movements around the dockside in a model such as this. As railway modellers we often choose to ignore the loads carried by the wagons and I find this quite curious. When I built a small oval layout for my young daughter's 'Thomas the Tank Engine', it was noticeable that one of her main interests in operating the layout was taking passengers and farm animals for trips around the layout. We look on this now with the amused tolerance of the superior modeller, but we hardly ever try to model the movement of real loads on a layout ourselves. I wonder why?

One of the nice things about this type of plan is how easily it can be set in different time periods and/or several different regions. You could run it as a North Eastern station around 1900, or a GWR layout of the 1930s, or a BR one in the steam era, depending on how you feel each day. With a few more weeds and the

Plan 3.6
Curdsmouth
(freelance)

1 Harbour
2 Road
3 Stone cottages
4 Hidden sidings
5 Goods shed
6 Loading dock
7 Public house
8 Ground frame
9 Up starter
10 Catch point
11 Platform
12 Station building
13 Cattle pens
LG Loading gauge

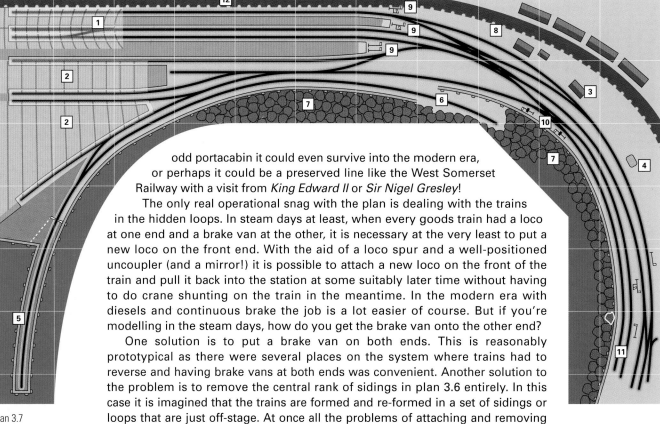

Plan 3.7

Penzance

1 Train shed
2 Canopy over
   goods platform
3 Signalbox
4 Water tower
5 Dock
6 Seawall sidings
7 Seawall with
   rocks
8 Retaining wall
   for main road
9 Up starter
   signals
10 Down siding
   signal (with
   descriptor
   display)
11 Carriage sidings
12 Low relief road
   and backscene

odd portacabin it could even survive into the modern era, or perhaps it could be a preserved line like the West Somerset Railway with a visit from *King Edward II* or *Sir Nigel Gresley*!

The only real operational snag with the plan is dealing with the trains in the hidden loops. In steam days at least, when every goods train had a loco at one end and a brake van at the other, it is necessary at the very least to put a new loco on the front end. With the aid of a loco spur and a well-positioned uncoupler (and a mirror!) it is possible to attach a new loco on the front of the train and pull it back into the station at some suitably later time without having to do crane shunting on the train in the meantime. In the modern era with diesels and continuous brake the job is a lot easier of course. But if you're modelling in the steam days, how do you get the brake van onto the other end?

One solution is to put a brake van on both ends. This is reasonably prototypical as there were several places on the system where trains had to reverse and having brake vans at both ends was convenient. Another solution to the problem is to remove the central rank of sidings in plan 3.6 entirely. In this case it is imagined that the trains are formed and re-formed in a set of sidings or loops that are just off-stage. At once all the problems of attaching and removing brake vans and locos are removed because they aren't seen. All that is modelled is the movements from the sorting sidings to the warehouse or factory or dockside.

Another way to avoid the need for a fiddle-yard is to turn the layout into an out-and-back layout, and where the station modelled is a main line terminus like Penzance (plan 3.7) this is often the best solution. The track plan is compressed to fit an 11ft room but is otherwise as accurate as I can get it, considering that none of the published plans I have seen match the photographs properly! The only deliberate change has been to replace the scissors crossing near the water tower with a plain crossover to make construction easier using off-the-shelf points. The large-radius curved points and single-slips from Peco are particularly useful.

Penzance has seen several changes over its lifetime but the plan is appropriate for the period 1939 to 1970-ish. The dock line and sidings disappeared gradually through the 1970s and 80s and the signals were simplified and then replaced by colour lights in 1982. The train shed lost its wooden front around 1960 and was rebuilt in 1990, but otherwise the plan is still relevant to today. The odd-looking siding close to the sea wall was put there in the 1950s to load stone onto the foreshore when the sea wall was rebuilt, and lingered on for a while before being lifted.

The original semaphore signalling was unusual in having full-size home signals for regular shunting moves including those into and out of the down sidings. The three down signals in the station all had mechanical descriptors on the post, which showed the intended path as an alternative to a lot of separate shunting arms. If you are up to the scratch-building task these would make a neat addition to the layout. All four platforms were signalled for arrivals and departures and each had its own up starter, and there were also main line starters by the scissors crossover plus an advance starter after the up spur.

Of course one of the reasons that a main line terminus is so rewarding to operate is the intensive activity it often sees. Some seaside termini such as Penzance and Weymouth Harbour would get so much seasonal traffic in broccoli or tomatoes that the entire station would be clogged with vans, and of course at other times they would be full of excursion trains. With its busy timetable of main line trains Penzance cannot sensibly be operated with a conventional fiddle-yard; unless you provide another terminus for the far end of the journey it will need a set of storage loops, either with a turntable and a well-thought-out track arrangement as in the plan of Glasgow St Enoch, or else a folding or removable reverse loop for operating sessions as suggested for Charlotte Street.

Now if you live a long way from the South Coast and are looking askance at the absence of seaside resorts further north, I have an apology. The plain fact is that the GWR region is covered by at least six major plan books which between them cover almost every GWR station one might be inclined to model, and most of the interesting stations are also captured in high-quality photographs from almost every conceivable angle. The SR and LMS each boast two books which, though almost as good as the GWR ones, leave many interesting stations unmapped or tantalisingly uncertain in critical aspects. And as for the LNER – well, I really have no idea why the region is so badly catered for in equivalent books and I have simply failed to find decent plans and photos of many of the locations that I would like to have included.

I did look through plans of several seaside stations in the North and Midlands, but the very closeness of the resorts to large population centres made them so popular as to need stations too large to make an accurate model practicable, or else the cities themselves were on the coast and hardly needed

Penzance in the late 1970s with a pair of large-logo class 50s on the 21:35 Paddington Sleeper. The Brunel train shed looks bare without its fascia and the goods yard has now been closed. With its awnings removed this gives a clear view of the goods platforms and tracks. (Photo S. Widdowson)

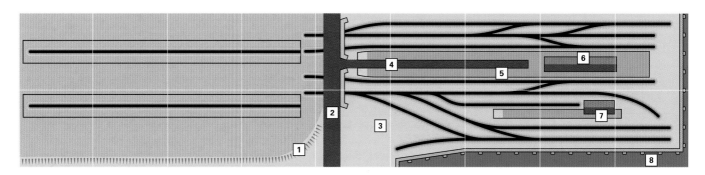

Plan 3.8

Kyle-of-Lochalsh

1 Hill
2 Road
3 Cattle Dock
4 Ramp to station
5 Platform
6 Station building
7 Goods shed
8 Estuary

the kind of picturesque small termini that Cornwall and Devon provided. So if you are an ardent modeller of the Northern scene I hope you will take my last two plans in this chapter in commiseration, both of which are in Scotland.

The railways were very late exploring Scotland and both 'iron roads' to the isles arrived there a good half-century after many lines in England. The station at Kyle, or Kyle of Lochalsh as the railway grandly described it, was built by the Highland Railway in 1897 and passed to the LMS at the grouping. It fell into BR hands in 1948 and is still, a little surprisingly, alive to day though now lacking its dock lines.

With its broad pier extending into Loch Alsh, Kyle is well suited to a compact model and the overbridge and rocky hillsides make natural visual breaks which allow the far end of the station to be replaced by a fiddle-yard (plan 3.8). The cassette type is a good choice here as it allows trains to access several lines independently and simultaneously. As drawn, the layout is pretty minimalist though very operable; with more space the surrounding scenery could be portrayed better as well as the rest of the station trackwork and I would certainly try to leave room for a ship or two at the dockside.

Another West Highland line of great scenic interest ran from Fort-William to Mallaig. The line was built with a government grant for the benefit of the fishing industry but its fame as a tourist line prompted the LNER briefly to run through-

Plan 3.9

Mallaig

1 Rocks
2 Boatyard and
   slipway
3 Signal cabin
4 Buildings
5 Church
6 Platform with
   cattle pens
7 Inspection pit
8 Turntable
9 Coal stage
10 Engine shed
11 Platorm
12 Platform canopy
13 Station building
14 Road

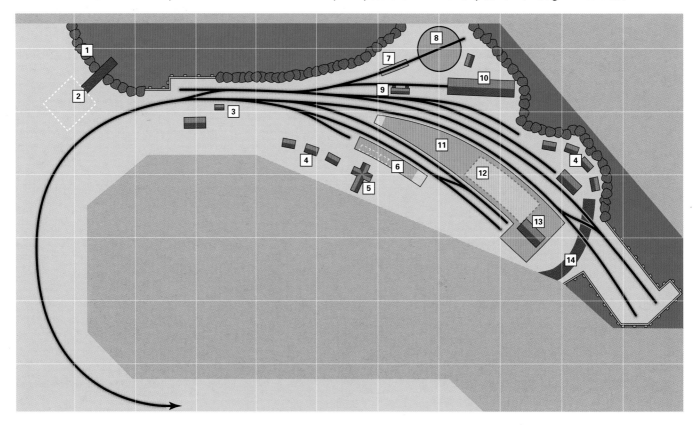

sleepers from King's Cross, though they later terminated at Fort William. The LNER also operated rail cruises in the 1930s and observation cars operated there into BR days, though with Class 27 diesels instead of steam.

As this line is still in existence, and still operated by steam in the summer months at the time of writing, on this layout I have attempted to model both the station at Mallaig and some of the scenery on the line (plan 3.9). As drawn, the plan fits into a space roughly 7ft by 11ft but would look good as an island in a much larger space where visitors could see it better and where the operator could walk around it. I have shown the baseboard significantly bigger than strictly necessary because the sea and rocks around the line are part of the atmosphere.

One of the interesting differences between Highland termini and the Southern resorts we looked at earlier is the proportion of passenger to goods traffic. Even on the road to the isles there was simply never enough passenger traffic to match the intensive holiday excursions of South West England. However, in the wild open Scottish Highlands where the long, twisty and narrow roads deterred road competition right up to the 1970s, what there was plenty of was freight, both general goods and fish, as is evident in both Kyle and Mallaig.

This 1974 view of Kyle of Lochalsh with 26032 heading an Inverness train shows how much of the station remained intact into the modern era. Although the distinctive SR van ahead of the coaches has wandered well outside its expected region this was surprisingly common in BR times. Note the sharp edge of the concrete paved section, the odd-length sleepers and lack of ballast on the adjacent track, though the platform line has clearly been re-ballasted. (Photo G.A. Watt)

Watching the Trains Go By

We are very fortunate today to have such a wide range of superbly detailed main line locomotives and coaches available ready-to-run in '00' gauge, 'N' gauge and even '0' gauge. Many modellers will, like me I am sure, have ended up buying many more of these than they can really find space for on their layouts.

This is particularly true of the branch-line terminus-to-fiddle-yard layouts that many modellers choose, since most of these branch lines never ever saw express locomotives in normal service. And on the busier seaside termini we looked at in the last chapter, which certainly did see express locomotives, we have the tricky problem of turning these trains around at the other end of the line in our fiddle-yard. There are of course several means of solving this problem, most of which we will see demonstrated somewhere or other in this book, but the classic solution to these problems is the continuous-run layout.

The great feature of these layouts is that having a continuous run of one or (often) two tracks in the form of an oval, it is possible to work an express locomotive with a full-length train up to a high speed at which it looks impressive. Although the basic form of this is often disparaged as a glorified 'train-set oval' or 'tail-chaser', it can make a realistic layout. When the tracks are run around the walls of the room and both the operators and viewers are inside, the sharp radii are much less obvious and annoying than when those same curves are seen from outside the layout as often happens at exhibitions. There are two main reasons for this: firstly we tend to turn our heads or bodies to follow a train around the room and thus keep it a more or less constant distance from us which gives the psychological impression of being further away, and secondly because the loose couplings of a model express train (which look so bad when opening up a tight curve) tend to close up when seen from inside the curve.

Plan 4.1

Country Station (freelance)

1 Privately owned factory
2 Gate
3 Signalbox
4 Platform
5 Station yard
6 Platform shelter
7 Station building
8 Goods shed
9 Goods platform
10 Road
11 Window
12 Door
13 Scenic break

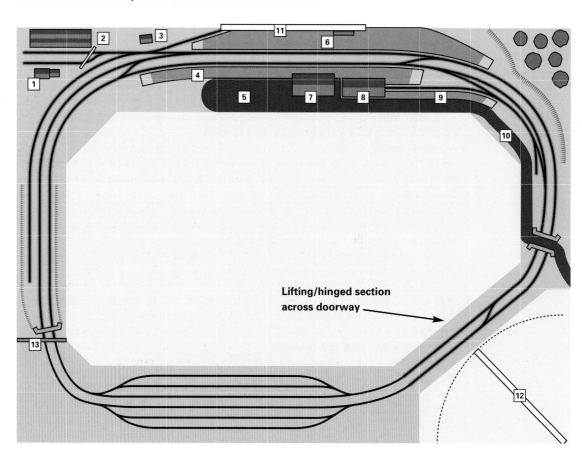

Therefore, although I know that many finescale exhibition modellers shun any radius less than 5ft for their exhibition layouts, it is quite acceptable in my view for a home modeller with a round-the-walls layout to use radii as small as 2ft around the corners, especially if the sharp radius can be disguised with a road overbridge. This enables a quite reasonable length of straight or near-straight main line to be presented along the longer walls of even a moderately sized room, which can if desired be used for a station. In my view straight track sections and those with reverse curvature are important to give the right impression, and using maximum radius curves can turn even a large layout into a train-set oval if one is not careful.

Plan 4.1 shows one such layout which is fitted into a room of 8ft x 11ft. The basic plan can, if necessary, be compressed into a much smaller space still, such as very small bedroom, and as the baseboard needs to be only 12in wide around much of the room and 18in at the widest, it can easily be fitted on a shelf above beds and drawer units with perhaps a hinged or lift-off section at the doorway.

The station is a freelance design but is fairly typical of many country stations throughout the country. Among its features are a loop with a platform for goods, a goods shed, and a cattle dock at the other end of the station, though the actual layout of these features could be criticised on several counts; for example the goods shed is much more commonly found on the loop rather than on a spur of it, for reasons discussed in a later chapter, though many examples can be found like this especially in the North East.

I have included a long siding which was found very often at countryside stations on main lines, in order to allow slow trains (usually freights) to set back into the siding to keep out of the way of faster trains. Through most of the steam days the vast majority of non-passenger trains conveyed short-wheelbase loose-coupled wagons or vans without continuous brake, and most of these were limited to a speed of 25mph and on very informal timings. This is perhaps why so many elderly locomotives survived for so long on goods trains – the slow speed and frequent stops left plenty of time for them to plod along and for the boiler to recover from the sudden effort required.

When electrically-powered point motors became more common on the full-size railway many of these sidings were converted into loops; they could not have been made this way when built in the 19th century because the point at the far end of the loop would have been too far away to pull from the signalbox. But many were left in their original form and for a layout like this the time and effort needed to reverse the train into the loop together or shunt the occasional pick-up goods can make an interesting and realistic piece of operation.

Another feature added to the plan to help this is the private siding. This could be any kind of private business but if you choose a specific one then you can plan the traffic it will need. If it is a factory as suggested here this will include raw materials in and finished goods out (probably in closed vans, perhaps with their maker's name on the outside – bicycles, prams, pots or pans?), plus coal or coke wagons in and empties back out. Scenically I have included cuttings to give variety and provide a suitable visual break for the end of the scenic section.

The area that is not scenic can be treated in many ways, and what you put here dramatically alters how the layout can be operated. Many beginners to railway modelling would be tempted to continue the scenic main line through this area to give a double-track continuous run all the way around the room. This certainly gives the maximum viewing area for trains but the operational possibilities are very limited – little better than a basic table-top train set, as trains run around and around in view with not much change. In order to change a train you have to remove it from the track bodily by hand; this is not only time-consuming but, with the latest super-detailed models, you will end up damaging them.

I much prefer to use a set of hidden storage loops instead, which can store several complete trains out of sight and let them run along the main line one after another with a very simple change of train via remotely controlled points. These allow a realistic sequence of trains to pass the operator/viewer without distraction and without much time needed to set up each train. Unfortunately storage loops take more space than cassettes because of the fan of points needed at each end. Curved set-track points can help, but when you have fitted long enough loops and a nice country station into a small room there may not be much room left for a decent main line as well. So why not leave the station out entirely?

If your fondest memories are of sitting by the lineside watching trains go by, or your main interest is in building or detailing rolling stock, then a continuous run with storage loops like plan 4.2 provides plentiful scope for scenery. It is easy to build and works well in the home, but has equally been the basis of some exceptional exhibition layouts including 'Holiday Haunts' and 'Stoke Summit'. To be sure, one has lost the ability to do shunting but if that doesn't interest you much then it's quite permissible to model a stretch of main line that is more typical of the bits we used to see from bridges over the line or nearby hillsides.

And speaking of scenery, I expect everyone who has travelled by train has at some time been fascinated by the way in which the railway line alternately rises above the surrounding landscape and sinks below it. To achieve this effect in plan 4.2 the ground drops away to show off the train at its best on an embankment but further around the ground rises again to let the train disappear momentarily from sight. Notice that we don't actually have to make the track itself climb – it is the land that rises and falls, and we can let the baseboards slope even if the line itself is level. The most extreme version of this is the drop-section with viaduct shown in front of the window, which not only helps to let the light through but is removable for window cleaning.

Plan 4.2 uses bridges to provide visual boundaries for sections of the layout, allowing different scenes to be displayed around the layout and making it look bigger. An overbridge in the corner also disguises the sharpness of the curve. A little thought will produce many variations on this theme once the strait-jacket of the conventional station has been dispensed with and one has made the conscious decision not to use flat baseboards!

Plan 4.2

Open country

1 Field
2 Viaduct
3 River
4 Road
5 Scenic break
6 Cottages
7 Window
8 Door

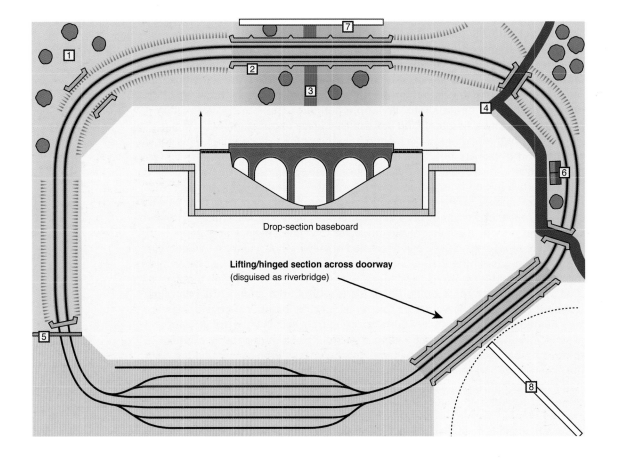

Drop-section baseboard

Lifting/hinged section across doorway
(disguised as riverbridge)

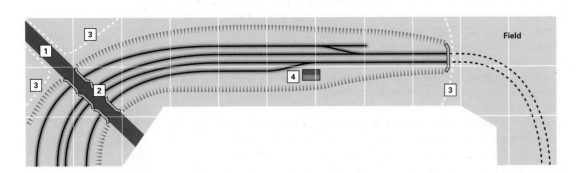

Plan 4.3
Stoke summit

1 Road
2 Viaduct
3 Fence
4 Signalbox

A continuous-run layout of this kind needs a significant storage capability since the majority of trains will pass through unchanged. One will need at least four trains in each direction to avoid too obvious repetition and would benefit from more. In a compact layout with a two-track main line this would require at least eight storage loops (four in each direction) and if we allow 2in per track in either '00' gauge or 4mm scale, this means at least 16in, which will need the whole baseboard width. If there is enough length to store two trains end-to-end this would need only half the width, though this is usually not possible in a small room without some trickery as we shall see later on.

Plan 4.3 is my take on Stoke Summit, shortened to suit a small room. If you don't think Stoke has really enough in the layout to be worthwhile modelling, then you probably haven't had to fight your way through thick crowds to view the Wolverhampton Club's wonderful exhibition model of this location.

For plan 4.4 I have taken as my inspiration the Scottish main line north of Edinburgh where it hugs the coast between Aberdour and Kirkcaldy, though the plan could quite easily be adapted for a favourite location elsewhere. I have shown a small passing station in one corner of the scenic section, which could

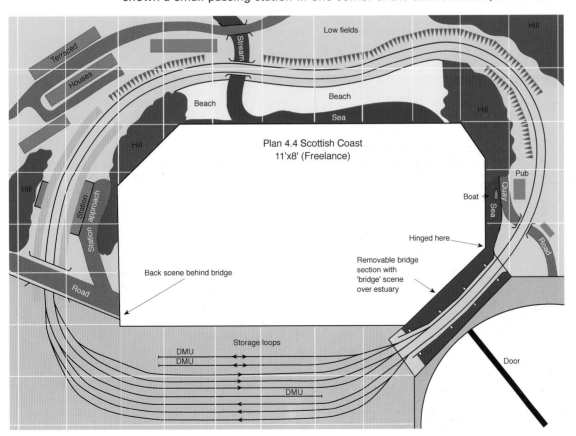

Plan 4.4 Scottish Coast
11'x8' (Freelance)

Plan 4.4
**Scottish Coast
11'x8' (Freelance)**

easily be deleted if preferred but serves to feed the small town behind the railway line. I feel that on a layout such as this, where most trains stop only briefly, there is no need to try to portray the whole station and several good reasons not to do so; it will either end up dominating the layout in a way it should not, or else it will look too short when a passenger train stops there.

A road overbridge disguises the entry to the hidden storage loops and also hides the end of the platforms to save space; a full-length train can stop half in view at the platform and then continue into or out of the storage loops. I have shown only three through storage loops in each direction as DMU services would rest in the dead-end sidings. More loops would be better but however many you choose, I can almost guarantee you will not have enough! Both the exhibition layouts mentioned above had lovely scenery but fairly plain trackwork on the section in view, and both had very large storage loops on which many trains could be stored and on which a small army of operators could change the locomotives and re-shuffle the trains. This was very effective for an exhibition layout but on a home layout which has much less space this may not be what you want. If it isn't, then there are a number of alternatives of which one of my favourites is to take the hidden storage loops by the scruff of the neck and make them look like something rather prettier.

An attractive prototype to choose for this is York which, with its long platforms and overall roof, is ideal for train storage. Plan 4.5 shows how this might look. You can see the station really dominates the layout, as you might expect in a room of only 8ft x 11ft, and will easily house those long-distance express trains that you will want to model. The station trackwork is compressed as always but I think the result does capture the essence of this great station. In a bigger space I would leave the station alone and have more main line scenery.

With its four bays there is also plenty of scope for the shorter-distance passenger trains. I suggest the back bays are used mainly for DMUs but the front ones have run-round facilities to suit steam power. Short hidden loops on

Plan 4.5
York Station

1   Hidden tracks
2   Road
3   Turntable
4   Coal
5   Ash
6   Station building
7   Occupation
    tunnel
8   Hinged bridge
9   Engine shed
10 Goods sidings
11 Embankments

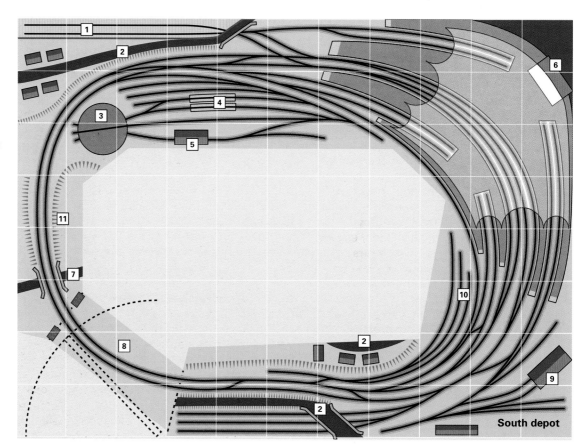

South depot

the 'Scarborough' line can hold 3- or 4-car DMUs and these can either run into the adjacent bay or continue on around the layout, and as facing and trailing crossovers are included at both ends of the station access to all bays is possible. Note that express trains would be expected to slow down as they passed these even if they do not stop. As drawn, the layout is intended mainly for passenger operation but with carriage sidings and two loco depots there is plenty of scope for prototypical operations such as change of locomotive and strengthening and shortening of rakes. The overall roof will be a challenge to make but will be essential for realism and worthwhile.

Goods facilities are frankly poor, the yard being included mainly for its visual effect. However, it is easy to improve on this by turning the South Depot into a goods yard and the far right-hand bay into a parcels platform. In this case I would also turn one of the carriage sidings into an up goods loop and run the South Depot headshunt into a slip on the other sidings to make shunting easier.

When designing a layout it is tempting to list a set of requirements such as 'must take 8-coach trains' but this can be a mistake if it limits the choices too much in the space available and prevents you appreciating the compromises that are necessary in a model layout. I much prefer to take inspiration from the prototype and see how much of it I can fit into a given space. If the answer is 'not enough' then I either choose another prototype or change it to a fictional setting.

To the modeller who prefers to model a real location rather than a fictitious one, the usual problem is finding enough space to fit in a realistic model of one's chosen prototype. This in turn often forces the modeller to avoid the type of location he would probably like to model and choose instead something much simpler. However, many of the most charismatic locations – King's Cross for example – were actually very cramped in reality and it doesn't take much work to fit them into a garage in 4mm scale as you will see in a later chapter.

The chief drawback of plan 4.5 as drawn is the short length of free main line on which the trains can run: they no sooner leave the station than arrive back. If the layout was transported into a larger room – say a large shed or garage – or the track was able to leave the shed for a route around the garden then this would be a great improvement. The other potential problem is that the station has inevitably taken over most of the room, and if the usual countryside scene is fitted along the far side of the room then there is very little room to show the inner-urban tangle of railway tracks and factories – the short region where the railway changed from being just another bit of track to being a real station.

I always found this part of the real railway fascinating but it is surprising how seldom modellers make a really good job of it. So often what is clearly a large city station just ends at the platforms and the train leaps immediately into serene countryside, whereas in reality there was usually a significant region of inner and outer-urban scenery each of which had its own character.

The inner-urban region was characterised by many small yards and depots, carriage sidings, etc, together with various factories most of which would in early steam years have been rail-connected but which gradually lost these connections over time. Indeed it can be nice to show lines that have been removed occasionally to convey this sense of changing purpose which is so much a part of city life. My plan of 'Hill Road' in Chapter 6 shows this part of the scene very well so I won't repeat it here.

The outer-urban region generally has much less railway infrastructure and more housing, and as cities grew outwards over time there would often be successive rings of Georgian houses and Victorian flats (often very tall), then late Victorian brick terraces, and finally the suburban 'semi' of the interwar period. Naturally the character of these regions would vary enormously between individual cities and parts of the country. This provides the chance to make your model specific to such a city or region rather than being simply generic. To show what I mean I have deliberately chosen the area around

Plan 4.6
Bristol

1   Office
2   Bath Road
3   Signalbox
4   Goods shed
5   Station building
6   Platform
7   Town scene
8   Coal
9   Turntable
10 Engine shed
11 Road
12 Window
13 Door

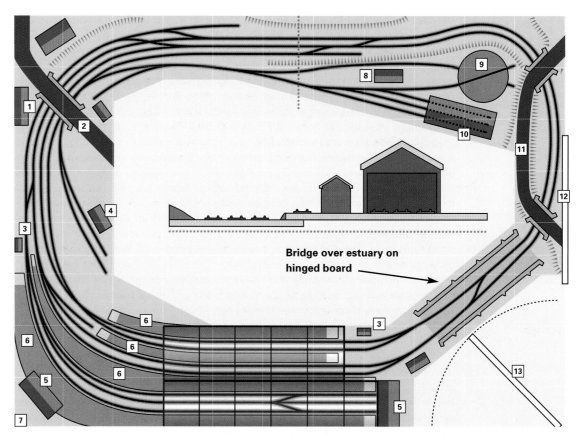

Bridge over estuary on hinged board →

Bristol Temple Meads as the inspiration for plan 4.6. However, although you could easily treat this as a model of that location, I did not intend that. Rather the model uses scenic elements from that station (including the Bath Road girder bridge) but arranged quite differently on the layout. This gives it a feeling of familiarity and yet novelty.

Another point worth making is that many people would automatically put a large station on the longest baseboard but I have avoided this here because I prefer to have a long main line there instead. So the station is instead on a curved site on the edge of the shortest baseboard. Once again you can terminate trains in the through platforms routinely to avoid the need for reverse loops, and as this forces you to change engines it is quite realistic.

The steam loco shed shown in the plan is intended to be added on at a later date as the layout grows, and I think it is very important on a home layout to allow room for it to grow like this. This is also why I do not favour building home layouts as accurate replicas of specific places – once the layout is complete there is nothing more to build. This is fine for an exhibition layout where you can sell it and build another one, but at home interest usually drops. The shed can hold a lot of engines and being an inch or so higher than the main line the new baseboard can be simply screwed on top of the old one with a slope for locomotive access. On a modern-image layout you could remove the turntable and replace it with a new shed and some oil storage tanks or a washing plant.

Goods facilities are limited so the layout as drawn will suit the lover of passenger trains best, though there is scope for parcel trains in both directions if the far terminal road is kept for parcels and arriving trains are reversed into it. But you could also model Pyle Hill goods depot (or indeed some private industry) in the space between Bath Road and the loco depot if you want.

Both the plans of Bristol and York would be greatly improved by another foot or two in width and perhaps a yard or so in length but, as you will appreciate, it is much easier to expand a plan than compress it, so I have deliberately left it in this basic size and left the expansion task to you. However, I would suggest that the main strengths and weaknesses of a plan like this would not be much altered by adding a few feet on each side.

Now when drawing these plans it is very tempting to make the rooms all different shapes and sizes and move the stations around the room for variety but there is always the suspicion that the designer chose the room to fit his plans instead of vice versa! This is why I have stuck with one size of room for many of these plans even where this is not ideal, to show how a given room – and even a built baseboard – can be modified over time to try several different layouts as one's interests and skills develop. It would not be difficult to build several of the layouts in this book in the same room as one changes one's views and aspirations.

As the plan of York showed, the main weakness in packing a large station into a small space is the lack of main line length for the trains to run on when they have left the station. This is, I'm afraid, the almost inevitable drawback of the simple oval railway line. However you try to disguise it, trains must either run around and around the layout repetitively or else they must travel a short distance and stop.

If you are lucky enough to have a large garage or purpose-built shed at your disposal then it is possible to get a set of hidden storage loops, a reasonable station and a nice length of main line into a round-the-room continuous run, but if you have much less space then this isn't possible.

Or is it?

There is a way to get more main line length into a continuous-run layout and if you will excuse the theatrical build-up, it is one worth exploring – the multi-level layout. Now I know there are those to whom the idea of running a railway line twice around a room is something they would never consider doing on grounds of realism, but I would urge the idea to be taken seriously since it offers a neat solution to many of the problems facing us.

Take the famous Lickey Incline, for example. This is one of many inspirational scenes but one I have never seen reproduced on a model layout. If one wants to make an acceptable model of a location like this then one will need the following features:

- the station at the start of the interesting scenic section;
- the scenic section itself, in this case the bank;
- a decent-sized set of storage loops to hold trains;
- room to show the scenery in convincing detail.

Though this would make an excellent subject for a large exhibition layout, it is difficult to see how this could all be managed in a basic oval that would fit into a normal-sized and -shaped room. But if we use the folded figure-of-eight layout, as in plan 4.7, it all fits into an 11ft x 8ft room very nicely. The station is modelled on Bromsgrove and although it has been altered heavily to fit the space available, it still provides facilities for banking which are usable on the model. The incline is again shortened in length but trains reaching the top do not immediately disappear into a tunnel. They have space to continue around the layout further before dropping down to base level again to enter the storage loops.

Now, to me, the section of scenery in which one railway line crosses over another is a dramatic one which I value for its own sake quite apart from its essential need in a folded-eight; with only a little care in electrical sectioning it is possible to get trains crossing over each other which is always a fascination on model and real railway alike. I also like seeing trains running in the background while I am operating a section in the foreground but if you don't like this then the descending line at the rear of the layout could be hidden behind a false backscene or even put in a tunnel.

However, an important benefit of leaving the line in view here is that it allows trains to remain in view for a longer time which I always enjoy. Now I know some modellers are happy to operate a station and don't care if the trains

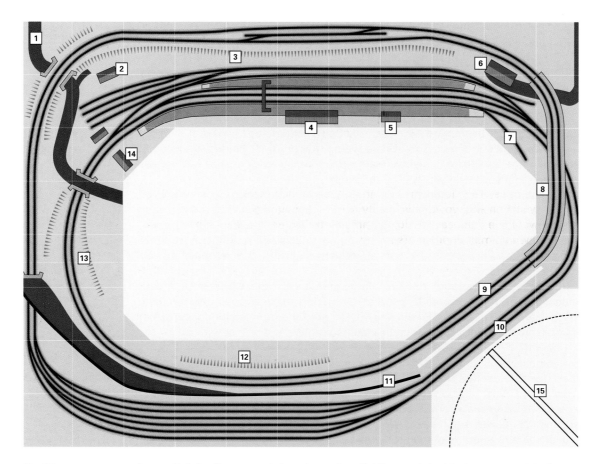

Plan 4.7

Lickey Incline

1 Road
2 Yard
3 Embankment
4 Station building
5 Signalbox
6 Hotel
7 Coal/ash pit
8 Viaduct
9 High level bridge
10 Low level bridge
11 Backscene
12 'Lickey incline'
13 Cutting
14 Houses
15 Door

immediately disappear into a tunnel or fiddle-yard, but I always want to know where the trains goes afterwards! Perhaps it is because I spent more time as a child travelling by trains than standing by the lineside watching them, but I like to follow a train around a layout, over bridges and through cuttings. If you like this too then the folded-eight may be for you.

In LMS days pairs of 'Jinties' provided most of the banking on the Lickey though various other locos were also tried. Banking locos used to wait in the central loops at top and bottom of the incline but in latter days the one at Bromsgrove was used as a down fast line and the siding at the other end of the station was used for bankers. If you are building this layout note that only the goods sidings are flat, though they weren't on the prototype! Everything else is on a gradient: 1 in 100 through the station and storage loops, 1 in 48 elsewhere. The real Lickey bank rose at a gradient of 1 in 37.7 but I wouldn't recommend copying this unless you are prepared to bank almost every train. A backscene is used to hide the storage loops but they could be covered by a removable scenic baseboard if preferred.

Another good reason to adopt a multi-level layout is the excitement of seeing trains from different regions crossing over one another. This happened in many places, including the picturesque viaduct at Midford where the Somerset & Dorset ran over the GWR branch line to Camerton, immortalised in the opening scene of the Ealing film *The Titfield Thunderbolt*. This is ideal for the person who can't quite decide whether he is a GWR or SR fan, or perhaps likes to run both LMS and LNER trains. So plan 4.8 has two entirely separate circuits at different levels, each running to a set of storage loops on one side of the room.

The original design was intended purely for watching the trains go by, with non-scenic storage on two levels. Access to the hidden loops would be by lifting off the brick retaining wall, and if 8-9in is allowed between rail levels there is easily room for hand access. However, it is a pity not to have some operation interest as well if only to create more variety, so it evolved into the plan shown. The first change was to make the upper track wind its way around the side of hills while the lower one disappears behind the hill. When one has so little length of main line to show it may seem perverse to hide any of it but to me this improves the scene and makes the layout look bigger.

The next change was to make the upper line swap between double track and single track part away around the layout. This has two purposes: to add variety to the main line below, and to give a reason why trains would need to stop in view while they wait for the single-line token or hand it back. The single-track section is very short, but there are various excuses for this. It could have been double track through two single-bore tunnels until one of the bores collapsed, or the girder bridge might have been de-rated to take only one loco at a time, or else a landslip forced the line to be singled. Or you could simply carry the single line further around the layout.

The upper storage loops in the plan also found themselves re-configured as a busy city station and would have plenty of low-relief buildings behind and to each side. It would be quite easy to do the same for the lower-level station but instead I have drawn a small goods marshalling yard instead, of the type often found on the edges of large cities where several routes converge. So for example GW and London Midland Region trains could each call at the yard to swap wagons, while Southern or North Eastern trains run past at high level. A system of shuffled cards can be used to determine the destination of wagon loads if desired to create interest.

Trains on the lower level would leave the hidden low-level storage loops, run around the layout through or past the marshalling yard, and then run on the main scenic section again before re-entering the hidden loops. With the marshalling yard and the goods loop there is now considerable opportunity to model prototypical train operation and this can ensure more fulfilment when the layout is complete.

When planning layouts with gradients the important question arises as to what gradient can be used, but unfortunately there is no definite answer. I have a forty-year-old Tri-ang 'Jinty' which will pull four period coaches up a 1 in 20 hill, but also a two-year-old 'Grange' class loco which after running in would still barely pull a scale-

Plan 4.8
Multi-level layout

1   Disused tunnel
2   Hill
3   Rocks/cliff
4   Embankment
5   Hillside
6   Disused line
7   High level
    bridge
8   Low level bridge
9   Signalbox
10   Station building
11   Retaining wall
12   Hotel
13   Door

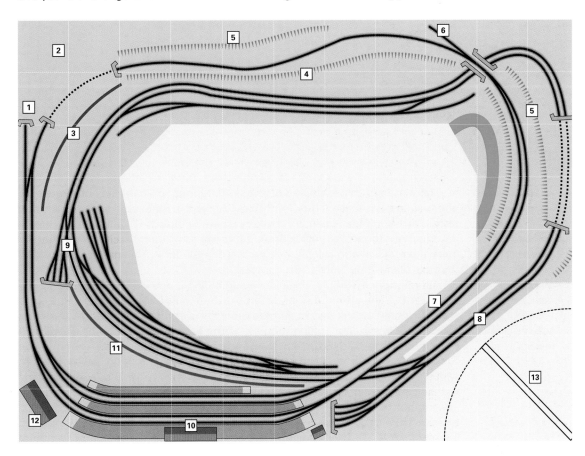

length train on the flat, though carefully degreasing the wheels and roughening the tyres with emery paper did improve things. Older models with tender drive and rubber tyres generally seem to climb hills much better, but this does mean you need to check gradients with the locomotives and rolling stock you intend to use.

Before building any layout with gradients I would suggest doing some loco haulage trials on a straight piece of track on a plank of wood, inclined on blocks. A good guide is that a train needs roughly twice its own length to climb its own height and getting on for three times its own length for clearance over another line. So with ruling gradients of 1 in 48 in plan 4.7 the 24ft circumference of the track plan will allow a 4in climb with trains of around 5 to 6ft long. This distance can be halved if the lower line drops as well but you must remember that sharp curves will add friction too, so minimum radius curves must be flat and level.

When you work out the maths you find that it isn't always possible to get a multi-level continuous-run layout into a small room without exceeding the gradient that the trains will manage reliably. An effective solution is to restrict the gradients to a branch line that runs from a small country junction to a high-level terminus situated above the storage loops. As the branch will see shorter trains and a more limited number of locos that can be hand-picked and weighted if required, it isn't too difficult to manage a gradient of 1 in 30 or less. And as many branches were really quite steep it would not be unrealistic for the engine to struggle slightly!

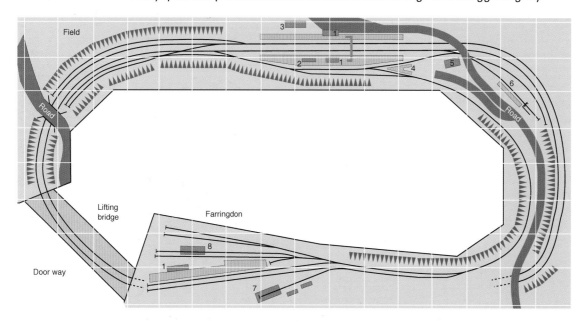

Plan 4.9
Uffington

1 Station building
2 Signal cabin
3 Pub
4 Milk dock
5 Station master's house
6 Loading dock & loading gauge

There are several examples of junction stations in Chapter 2, but here's an unusual one based on Uffington (plan 4.9) which connected with the branch terminus Faringdon we have already seen in plan 1.1. The line is nicely described in Adrian Vaughan's book *Signalman's Morning* and was so short (a mere three miles) and steeply graded that the model is not too far from reality. Here the plan is fitted into a 16ft garage.

Although the Faringdon branch closed in 1963, one could easily add a new platform by the up sidings at Uffington and operate the branch line as a preserved railway; this would suit the modeller with both modern image rolling stock and a few steam outline models, as the branch line can be operated as a preserved railway. Any express steam locomotive in preservation – even *Flying Scotsman* – could then justifiably run along the main line and up the branch, which it never would have done in the steam age. As it will still be running short trains on the branch it should still manage the gradient, but check first!

Another idea which I have shown fitted into the very small 7ft x 8ft third bedroom typical of many homes is to have a low-level quarry as the scenic interest (plan 4.10). There is a double-track main line, part of which is in a tunnel

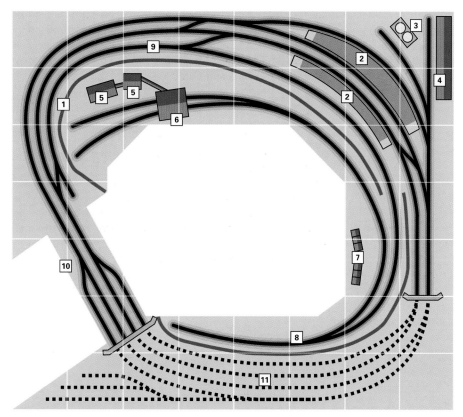

Plan 4.10
Quarry Layout

1 Quarry face/
  rock cliffs
2 Platforms
3 Oil tanks
4 Factory
5 Screening plant
6 Loading chute
7 Workers
  cottages
8 Quarry
  headshunt
9 Quarry
  reception
  siding/loop
10 Hinged bridge
11 Storage tracks
   hidden under
   tunnel

to disguise the small circle and allow the trains to go off-stage occasionally. Note how the track radius has been varied to create interest here, rather than attempting to use maximum radius curves everywhere.

But the key to the layout is the quarry, which is set at low level with a deliberately steep slope to justify the locomotive moving only a few wagons at a time up to the main line. I imagine a Class 59 locomotive here with a short rake of stone hoppers but the scene could equally be a coal mine or industrial site. For the modern-image freight enthusiast the layout provides an excellent opportunity for scenic modelling. The bridge over the doorway can be hinged on blocks just above rail level or can simply lift off. Note that it is important to allow the door to swing open wide enough to allow easy access.

With a room of this size it is difficult to get in a decent length of main line running, but not impossible, as the spiral layout in plan 4.11 shows. Spirals are not as popular here as in the USA but this one provides a 50ft main line run between a high-level city terminus and a low-level harbour station. Trains run two and a half times around the room on each journey. The stations are freelance but inspired by real places. Westcliffe (plan 4.11a) is based visually on Exeter Queen Street in steam days, where the main line dropped very steeply down between sidings to Exeter St David's below. Note how the cramped space between the buildings in the corner adds character which would be lost in a much larger space – larger is not always better!

Midchester is just a place for trains to pass one another but Oxmouth (plan 4.11b) at the other end of the line is obviously based on Weymouth Harbour, though the turntable and boatyard owe more to Kingswear. The layout suits trains of 4-5 coaches and these should be manageable on the ruling gradient of 1 in 48. Shunting the sidings at Westcliffe is best done off-peak when the platforms are both free but this complexity helps to make life interesting! The carriage sidings could be replaced by a timber yard or similar business if desired, and with the harbour would provide much opportunity for freight train movements.

This layout is unusual in using separate high- and low-level baseboards for the main stations. The lower baseboard is the only conventional one and construction must necessarily start here. The Westcliffe baseboard, a foot above this, is also fairly normal but the frames must be carefully placed to avoid the tracks below. The cutting on the opposite side of the room should be built lightly to avoid shielding the tracks below and I suggest it is angled to make the tracks more visible. The two bridge sections by the door are parallel but at different heights and both hinge up behind the door.

Plan 4.11a
Westcliffe

1   Station building
2   Platforms
3   Engine shed
4   Ash pit
5   Coal staithes
6   Turntable
7   Railway cottages
8   Road bridge
9   Warehouse
10 Carriage sidings
11 Cutting side
12 removable bridge to Oxmouth layout
13 Hill/tunnel

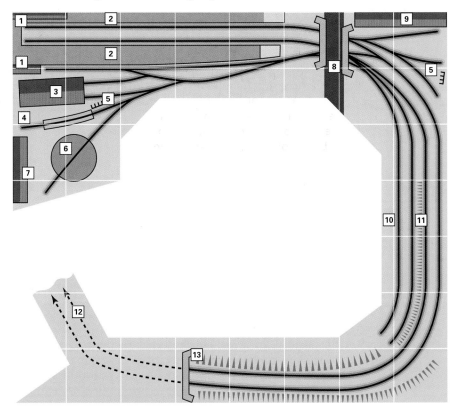

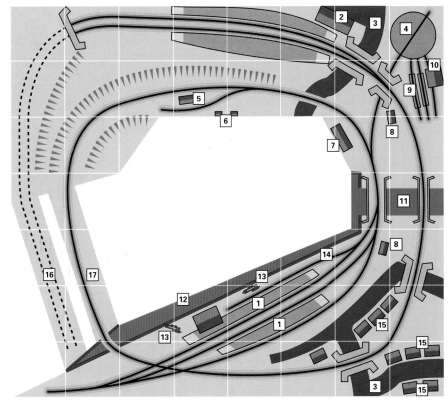

Plan 4.11b

Oxmouth & Midchester

1   Platforms
2   Station building
3   Road
4   Turntable
5   Factory
6   Sheds
7   Boatyard
8   Signalbox
9   Ash pits
10 Coal tower
11 River
12 Harbour
13 Cranes
14 Quay
15 Houses
16 High level bridge
17 Low level bridge

The Loco Shed

One of the most fascinating aspects of the steam-age railway was the steam locomotive itself – the huge iron beast that snorted fire and smoke, barked loudly when asked to work hard, and screamed unexpectedly in protest at being left idle for too long. For those of us who were either too young or too busy to visit the locomotive sheds we glimpsed in the distance, our closest view of the loco was usually standing by the platform edge as it waited patiently with its train.

But for the few sufficiently enterprising who attempted and succeeded in gaining entry to the holy temple of steam itself, going on shed was an experience that, in retrospect, seems so extraordinary we wonder how it could ever have been allowed at all. In an age long before health and safety legislation, before regulations on working conditions, and before any real worry about pollution, the steam shed was in many respects the last vestige of a bygone era. A century after gas lighting became common and a full half-century after electric power had been introduced, many sheds remained apparently free of any kind of artificial lighting at all.

The traditional steam shed seemed to combine the vast size and stygian gloom of the gothic cathedral with a combination of dirt, oil, water, and smells that occasionally seemed more redolent of hell. But to walk through it and actually touch the monsters we had so often seen straining at their couplings, and to find them quite still, silent, and as if frozen, was an experience that, once felt, was never forgotten.

But the curious thing is how few of us make any real attempt to model the shed in any detail, and that even fewer are really confident about how one operated. Much that was taken for granted in those now far-off days has become lost to memory.

I suspect for most railway modellers the primary purpose of a loco shed on a model is somewhere to turn our locomotives and store them until needed. As children we gaily stuck a Tri-ang or Hornby Dublo turntable on our 6 x 4 baseboards with a couple of sidings off it and called it a loco depot, unconcerned at what really went on there.

But today, when it seems every layout makes some pretensions to being both realistic and prototypical, and the model locomotives themselves have exceeded all expectation in detailing, we surely have some duty to try just a little harder to get things right.

GWR 2-8-0 No 3860 (one of the Collett locos with larger cab) poses in front of a typical double-sided Churchward coaling stage with a mixture of steel and wooden wagons on view. Although the coaling tubs are hidden the pair of pivoted tracks on which they run can be clearly seen folded up out of the way. (Ian Allan Library).

So where do we start? It is all very well wanting to model Old Oak Common or Haymarket shed, but there's little possibility of us achieving that in the small corner of the third bedroom we may have available.

Fortunately we don't have to. It should not be too much of a surprise to learn that just as the average railway modeller wants a place to turn and store a few locomotives next to his terminus without the bother of sending them far away, his full-size counterpart often wanted the same thing.

Both Paddington and King's Cross stations (plan 6.10) had a turntable close by them, though strictly speaking these weren't 'sheds' as they didn't have an allocation of locomotives or any repair facilities. Glasgow St Enoch did too (as you can see elsewhere in this book) and this actually did have a 'shed' attached. Then there were many smaller stations which had either a turntable or a shed, or both, attached to them, as a skim through the plans in other chapters will show.

The Southern Region did the same at Bognor Regis (plan 5.1) and surprisingly this survived electrification of the line serving the station, I presume to cope with the occasional steam-powered excursions and specials. This depot is an object lesson in prototypical minimalism, as it contains just the bare essentials we could all fit on our layout: a turntable, inspection pit, small coal stage, a small covered shed for basic maintenance out of the rain, and a bit of trackside where ash and char can be dumped.

Plan 5.1

Bognor Regis (SR)

1   Signalbox
2   Sand drag
3   Turntable
4   Ash pit
5   Engine shed
     (water tower
     over)
6   Station building
7   Low relief
     timber mill
8   Timber store
9   Loading dock
10 Platform

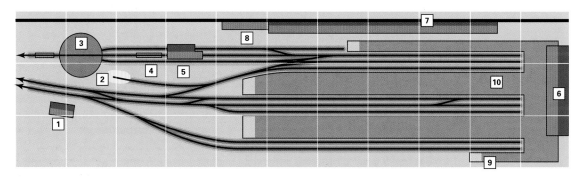

The station itself would make a nice model, especially if there is space to reinstate the sidings to the coal dumps and timber mill on the down side of the loco depot but more important is the proof that something this small and simple is prototypical.

Such depots are ideal for a small space but if you have many more locomotives you will need something bigger and will probably want to make a prototypical model of a shed, whether it is a real shed or a fictional one. This presents much more of a problem. Most of the real loco depots were much too large to copy accurately and they also varied enormously, so it isn't at all clear how they were used or which bits need to be kept in the model. Each of the railway companies had its own preferred style of shed though they also inherited a great many from previous companies.

The GWR had a strong corporate identity and in the first few years of the 20th century their chief locomotive engineer, G. J. Churchward, produced large numbers of sheds to a standard pattern. There were two main varieties of the standard shed – turntable sheds and straight sheds. Turntable sheds are sometimes called roundhouses though Churchward's were always square with a central turntable, usually 65ft, and typically 28 tracks leading from it in four groups of seven (see plan 5.2). Some, like Wolverhampton, had two of these turntables and a few, like Old Oak Common, had four in a square formation. They always shared some internal lines to ease the throughput of locomotives.

Even one of these sheds would need a square yard of space to do properly which is impractical, so if we want to build one we will have to cheat. One way to do this is to paint the roundhouse on the backscene which allows you make it as big or small as you want – plan 5.2 could be wrapped around a chimney-

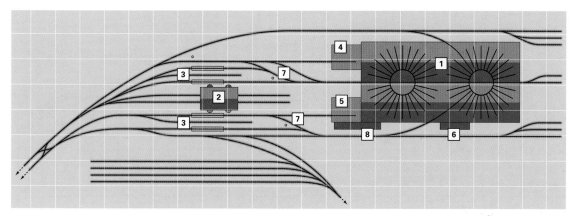

breast quite nicely! Locomotives stand around in view and never enter the shed at all unless you have room for a hidden siding behind the backscene.

Another way is shown in plan 5.3, which is my take on the 1907 depot at Aberdare. The roundhouse has been reduced in size to the width of a single turntable and I have used the repair shop and stores buildings to hide some of the turntable lines. If you don't have room for the lines at the far left-hand end of the building it can be chopped off short there. The rest of the plan is close to the original except the entry from the main line which has been simplified.

Plan 5.4 is based on one of the earliest Churchward standard straight sheds at Leamington, and is fairly accurate except for the entry to the coal sidings which has been moved to shorten the plan, and the carriage sidings which have been omitted as they obscure the coaling line. The facing point and crossover on the main line are unusual and would probably not have been used outside station limits where speeds were higher. But don't be misled by the 'standard shed' bit in the title – every shed was different! Straight sheds could be double-ended or single-ended, and the turntables could be placed anywhere. The entrance line to the shed also varied in position, and other buildings such as repair shops were added at various dates.

However, the GWR adopted a very distinctive coaling stage which was retro-fitted to many larger sheds and used a sloping ramp to raise coal wagons to the top of the stage, and a miniature track for coal tubs to run sideways to and fro between the coal wagon and the locomotive. The track had curved ends to it so that tubs could be up-ended without falling off (see photo on page 43).

The coaling stage supplied either one track or (if it was double-sided) two as in plan 5.2, and could be built in different lengths to supply several locomotives at once. A common feature of the GWR standard shed was the provision of two ash-disposal loops with points at each end and a dead-end siding between them where empty wagons could stand ready for ash to be shovelled into them. Some sheds didn't bother with this as the wagons could always be pushed onto the coaling line when the shed wasn't busy.

If you intend to build one of these, *An Historical Survey of Great Western Engine Sheds 1947* has some useful photos and drawings. Photos of the sheds

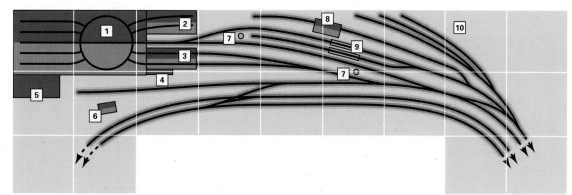

Plan 5.4

Leamington (GWR)

1   Shed
2   Turntable
3   Coal stage
4   Ramp
5   Ash pits
6   Coal sidings
7   Inspection pits
8   Water columns
9   Double slip

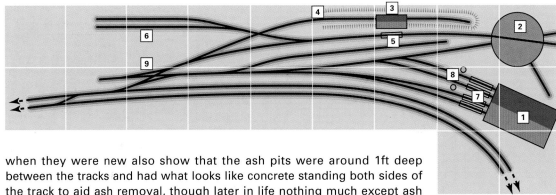

when they were new also show that the ash pits were around 1ft deep between the tracks and had what looks like concrete standing both sides of the track to aid ash removal, though later in life nothing much except ash would be visible.

To appreciate how a shed is used, it is best to follow a locomotive around Leamington depot (plan 5.4). On arrival at a large shed the crew manning the locomotive would usually sign off at the offices, often attached to the shed (1) and leave the locomotive somewhere convenient for the disposal crew. In a small shed like Leamington they could well drive the engine themselves to position (5) where the tender could be filled with coal, the ash could be emptied from the grate and the fire dropped. If necessary they might remove a firebar or two or just use the long-handled tools to clear the fire off the bars. At some point the smokebox door would also be opened and the char shovelled out.

The locomotive would then be driven along the track to the turntable (2) and turned if necessary, then driven back around the loop and reversed into the shed (1). Inspection pits (7) by the shed would allow driver or fitters to check and oil the motion, and water columns (8) nearby allow the tanks to be filled.

Although locomotive sheds varied enormously over the country, the process described was pretty similar. During the week steam locomotives were used pretty intensively and rarely had much chance to cool down between shifts. The photos you sometimes see of a shed absolutely clogged with locomotives nose to tail were usually taken on a Sunday when most of the shed's allocation of locos would be resting there. At many sheds locomotives spent their on-shed time sitting in the open, come rain or shine. Covered sheds were mostly provided for the comfort of the fitters who had to work on the locomotives to repair and maintain them, although if you visited one you wouldn't think comfort was very high on the company's agenda! But replacing axleboxes, piston glands, gauges and other sundry items was all best carried out under cover. For any more specialised tasks the locomotive would probably be sent to the company's main repair shops (Swindon, Crewe, Doncaster, etc).

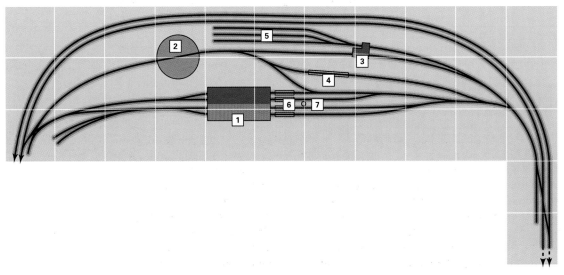

Plan 5.5

Carnforth c1951 (LMR)

1   Shed
2   Turntable
3   Coal stage
4   Ash pits
5   Coal sidings
6   Inspection pits
7   Water column

The LMS had a standard pattern shed which was fairly similar to the GWR straight shed as it had to do the same things, but the coaling stages varied more. Large loco depots in most regions had high coaling stages like the LMS one at Carnforth (plan 5.5) which involved raising wagons up and tipping them bodily into large hoppers. The GWR never used this as its favourite Welsh steam coal was too easily shattered into useless dust and it stayed with its low-drop method to the end. Some other regions also used a raised ramp to reduce the manual labour required to remove coal from wagons; the delightfully compact ex-LNWR shed at Coventry is a case in point (plan 5.6). In a smaller space this could be compressed still further into a two-road shed and the spur off the turntable missed out.

Turntables varied enormously: early ones were designed to take a six- or eight-wheeled locomotive and were often no more than 30-45ft in diameter. The one at Pencader (plan 2.5) was 28ft across! As locomotives increased in size during the early years of the 20th century so did the turntables and many sheds had several different turntables at various times in their history, often in different places. So if you're building a model take particular care with the dates of the plans and photos you use for reference and don't just assume they will be correct for your modelling period.

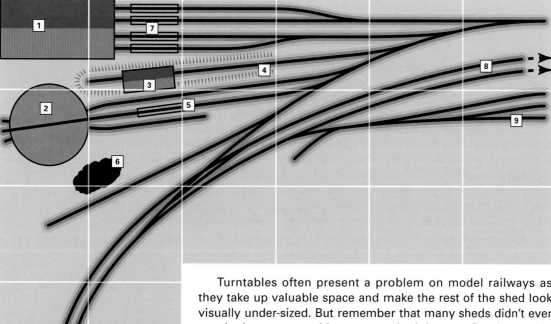

Plan 5.6

Coventry (LNWR)

1 Four-road shed
2 Turntable
3 Coal stage
4 Ramp
5 Ash pits
6 Coal heap
7 Inspection pits
8 Main lines
9 Carriage sidings

Turntables often present a problem on model railways as they take up valuable space and make the rest of the shed look visually under-sized. But remember that many sheds didn't ever get the largest turntables, so you don't have to fit a huge 12in turntable to your layout just because you can buy one in the shops – it's quite OK to make an 8 or 9in turntable yourself and send your 'A4' or '9F' off-stage to be turned.

Speaking of turntables, it isn't always appreciated how much time it took to turn a locomotive. To start with, the loco's wheelbase might not be much shorter than the turntable which made accurate positioning important. Occasionally it might even be longer, which required extension rails to be laid out and the tender driven up into the air on these. Even on a 70ft turntable, which might seem plenty long enough, balancing the loco could be critical to the task of pushing the turntable around with a 100-ton loco on top. Many turntables were hand-operated, some by a geared hand-wheel, though later ones were often operated either electrically or by vacuum, coupling up a hose to the loco. As a consequence, using a turntable to access sidings was a very slow process and although it saved on points, most companies preferred to stick it on a spur somewhere instead and use a fan of points to access the shed and sidings.

The other aspect of the shed which should be modelled if authentic operation is desired is the flow of coal and ash. Most loco depots had a fan of sidings for coal wagons and small groups of wagons would be shunted from these to the coal stage and back as required. Likewise other wagons would be shunted to and from the ash pits to clear these. I have deliberately included these on most of the plans so you can model this traffic properly. Photographic evidence of these activities is rare because most of them took place in brief periods when photographers weren't around, though I have seen a picture of a petrol-powered mechanical shovel lifting ash out of ash pits into a waiting wagon.

A few sheds had a trench into which a track was sunk for ash wagons so their tops were level with the ground, allowing ash to be shovelled directly into them, but most of the time I suspect human power was the norm. Remember that every shed had a place for ash removal. Note also that most sheds had inspection pits between the rails in the shed or just outside, but these were not supposed to be used for ash removal!

However, the vast majority of older and smaller sheds of the kind you might be able to fit next to a small station used much more primitive methods. The typical coal stage was little more than a wooden platform with a large bin (possibly made from old sleepers) into which coal would be shovelled by hand from an adjacent wagon. When the wagon was removed the stage was free for locos. If the fireman was lucky a small hand-powered crane would be available. If he wasn't he would have to shovel the coal into the tender himself. One or two sheds didn't even have this – they just left a full coal wagon on a convenient track, parked the locomotive next to it, and stood on the coal they shovelled into the locomotive's tender!

In pre-grouping days most companies used coal wagons specially marked 'Loco' to ensure the best quality coal got to their own locos and didn't get lost en route, but as time went by, ordinary wagons were used for this traffic and by the 1950s the ubiquitous 16-ton steel wagons were mostly used, both for coal and ash.

There are several other shed plans to be seen elsewhere in this book, both prototypical and freelance, but if you don't have room for a full layout and still love collecting locomotives, why not consider a shelf layout? The final two plans can be used either on their own, or with a small fiddle-yard, or could connect to a separate layout if desired. Both are freelance designs but can be operated properly, with the flow of locos around the shed and with the capability to shunt coal and ash wagons to and from sidings. Plan 5.7 is intended to represent an LMSR scene and plan 5.8 is typical of the GWR. Both of these have an entry from one end, though if extra width is available both could be modified to incorporate a central exit to sidings behind the backscene, and on plan 5.8 these should include coal sidings.

Plan 5.7 (below)
Shelf layout

Plan 5.8 (bottom)
GWR shelf layout

1　Shed
2　Turntable
3　Coal stage
4　Inspection pits
5　Ash pits
6　Mess room
　　(old coach body)
7　Stores/sand
　　furnace
8　Water column
9　Coal sidings
10　Water tower
11　Entry line to
　　shed

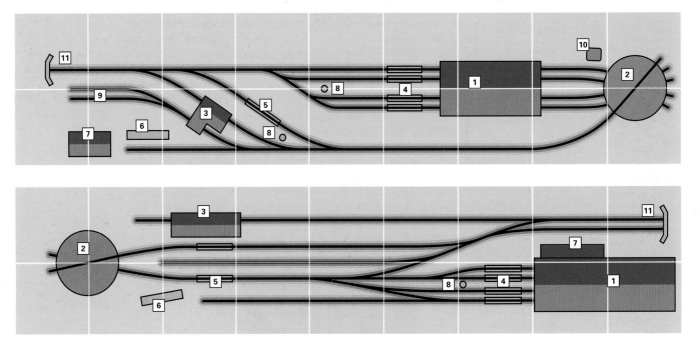

Modelling the City Scene

On the ever-popular country branch terminus layout it is difficult to justify an 'A4', 'Duchess' or '9F' locomotive unless you model it as a preserved railway. Most of them used a small range of tank locos for the majority of their history, and although you are free as a modeller to run what services you wish, it seems odd to pick a country branch for the sake of realism and then make up quite unrealistic services for it. In steam days most branch lines had very little traffic, which is of course why so many closed. Country stations were also nowhere near as small as people imagine; they were often built on the outskirts of a village on cheap agricultural land and included enough space for expansion that seldom occurred, so they usually sprawled over the landscape and without any strong visual breaks it is often difficult to capture the scene in a small space.

Plan 6.1
Charing Cross

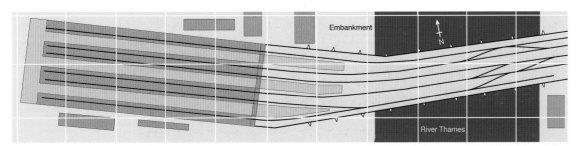

By contrast inner-city stations usually had to find expensive land in the city centre and by the time they wanted to expand they couldn't easily do so. Charing Cross, for example, was a very compact station (plan 6.1) and although the variety of operation did reduce when electricity took over from steam, it still saw plenty of action.

My next plan, Charlotte Street, (plan 6.2) is an entirely freelance design but one which is not all that far from several city stations in style. You may be surprised at the lack of run-round facilities, but most engines arriving at a city terminus in steam days didn't run round their train and leave again – they went 'on-shed' to be coaled and watered. If the stock was to leave immediately, a new loco would couple onto the back of the train and the original train engine would

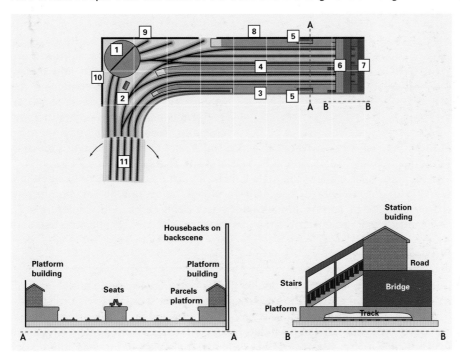

Plan 6.2
Charlotte Street Station

1 Turntable
2 Signalbox
3 Down platform
4 Up platform
5 Platform buildings
6 Station building
7 Road
8 Low relief station buildings
9 Tenement buildings
10 Railway offices
11 Swivelling train store

follow it out. It would then go to the turntable and sit on one of the spurs while the fireman cleaned the fire and ashpan. The turntable shown isn't a loco shed per se, but a servicing depot like those at Paddington and King's Cross where visiting locomotives could be turned, watered and inspected.

If the stock wasn't needed, it might either be shunted into another platform by the station pilot to release the train engine, or taken into the carriage sidings. As these are conveniently off-scene, the coaches will need to be brought back on-scene later in the day, and so a considerable variety of movements will be necessary for even one train, which greatly adds to the operating interest.

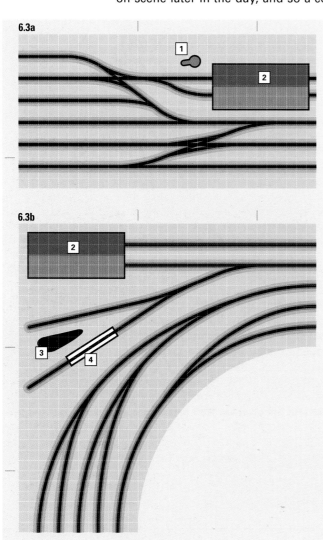

6.3a

6.3b

With low-relief or painted houses on the backscene and a high-level station building on the end, almost the whole of the station length can be used for train storage. The plan is only 8ft long in '00' but can take 5- or 6-coach trains; it can also hold five trains at once despite being only 18-20in wide. I suggest some low-relief railway buildings behind the turntable, but Paddington-style brick or cement-faced flats work just as well. The far platform could be for parcels.

The next question is where the trains go when they leave the station. Now I'm not a lover of fiddle-yards for reasons discussed earlier, so I have suggested a set of parallel storage lines on a swivelling baseboard. All of these are carried around to the station and represent the 'rest of the world' – a couple of fast lines, a goods/parcels line, a carriage/light loco line, etc. The table can be turned to line up different combinations, and to release engines from the ends of the storage roads back to the shed.

One of the good things about this kind of layout is how easily it can be expanded. If you have a little more space available you can add a new section of baseboard between the station and store as shown in plan 6.3a, and if this has enough points to allow trains to cross lines you may not need

Plan 6.3a & 6.3b

**Alternative
expansion boards**

1   Water tower
2   Engine shed
3   Coal
4   Ash pit

to make the train store swivel at all which saves a lot of hassle! In a 6ft x 8ft shed the corner adapter (plan 6.3b) might be useful and also expands the loco depot.

Like many such stations the main lines would all be signalled for bidirectional working in the vicinity of the station, which helps reduce the points and crossovers needed, and the down platform can easily be used for departure only. The nearside storage lines could then be used for DMUs, HSTs and auto-trains.

Reverse Loops

If more space is available I would take the opportunity to add in a reverse loop as this removes the need to release engines in the 'fiddle-yard' and lets you concentrate your attention where it belongs, in the station. If you are working in '00' gauge you will need at least 2nd radius curves to take the latest RTR locos which means a 3ft half-circle of track. You can make part of the loop fold up out

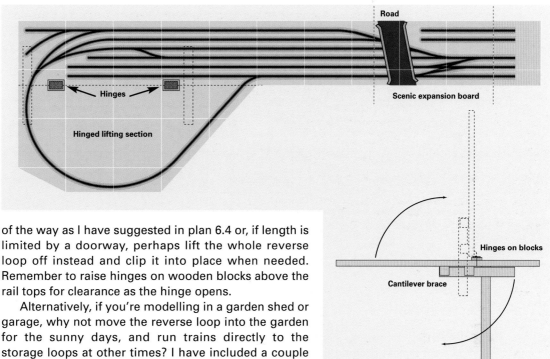

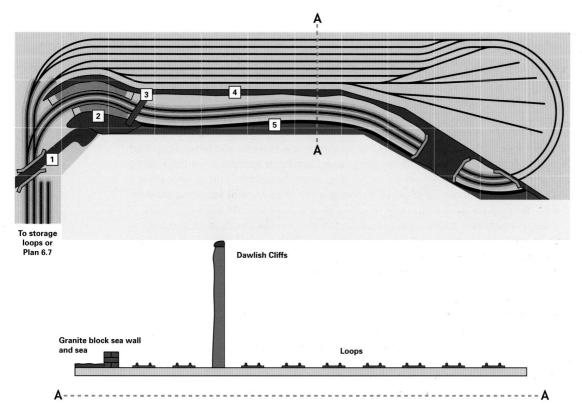

of the way as I have suggested in plan 6.4 or, if length is limited by a doorway, perhaps lift the whole reverse loop off instead and clip it into place when needed. Remember to raise hinges on wooden blocks above the rail tops for clearance as the hinge opens.

Alternatively, if you're modelling in a garden shed or garage, why not move the reverse loop into the garden for the sunny days, and run trains directly to the storage loops at other times? I have included a couple of dead-end roads for DMUs, HSTs, etc. You will notice that all trains leaving the terminus (except DMUs) run around the reverse loop before stopping in the storage loops. This makes it easy to change locomotives from the station.

If you have more space you can make the reverse loop double track and have it fully scenic, with the storage loops behind a backscene. Plan 6.5 shows the general idea, though this was originally drawn to go with the plan of Penzance (plan 6.7), and a mirror image would be needed here. The scene is obviously

Plan 6.4

Reverse loop and storage for city terminus

Plan 6.5

Dawlish and Teignmouth

1 Road
2 Hill
3 Footbridge
4 Cliffs
5 Granite sea wall and sea

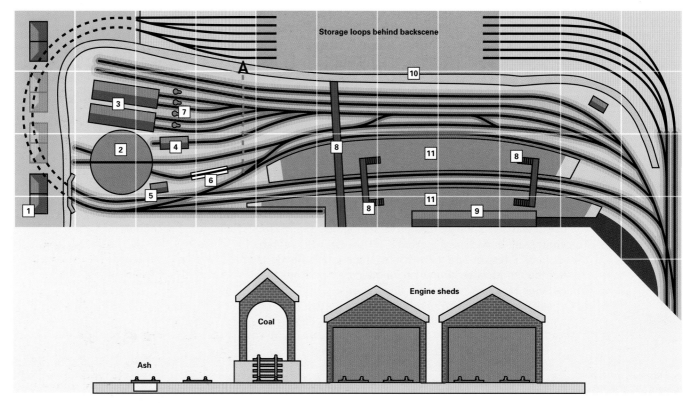

Plan 6.6

Truro Station

1 Semi-detached
   houses
2 Turntable
3 Engine sheds
4 Coal
5 Signalbox
6 Ash pit
7 Water towers
8 Footbridges
9 Station building
10 Cliffs backscene
11 Platforms

inspired by the Dawlish-Teignmouth stretch of GWR main line. I apologise for digressing from the city to yet another GWR coastal scene but when one is looking for an atmospheric scene that is pretty yet narrow, the natural tunnels and hills of this line are too good an opportunity to miss!

Another way of using the space in front of hidden storage loops to advantage is shown in plan 6.6. This started out very much like plan 6.5 but once I had pondered how to make the tunnel entry look realistic I remembered Truro and the layout grew a good-sized loco shed, platforms and even a couple of carriage sidings behind. Although the sidings are compressed quite heavily, the scene should be more than capable of standing scrutiny as Truro and there are plenty of photographs available in books to work from. The popular view of the shed shows the sheer cliffs behind the shed, with a nice row of 1930s semi-detached houses on the skyline which can be easily reprinted from photographs and stuck on the backscene.

There is just about room for a Churchward-style coal stage too, which is seldom modelled properly. The plan is shown as 11ft long, which suits a room of 11ft x 8ft or so in which the terminus is on the opposite wall next to the door, but both this and the terminus can be lengthened or shortened easily in the middle at the cost of changing the maximum length trains usable. However, I would stick to 2nd and 3rd radius set-track in the reverse loop itself as this maintains its shape better than flexitrack.

Many modellers today seem reluctant to model real locations, perhaps for fear of 'getting it wrong' but don't be put off. While preparing the Truro plan I checked several published track plans of the prototype from books and found them all quite different! The plan as shown is compressed as usual and the goods depot at the up end has been omitted entirely, but is it really any more 'wrong' than the actual pre-1904 layout (before the main line was doubled) or post-1971 layout (after the shed closed and the sidings were taken up)?

I feel it is very worthwhile working from photos and track plans of real railway scenes even if you do decide to deviate from them, or to give them a fictitious name and location, as the research is interesting in itself and helps one to understand the way the railway was actually worked. Modelling a section of real main line, with real stations, makes the traffic flow so much more realistic and this offsets the compromises necessary in the actual trackwork and scenic boundaries.

As an example of this, consider Penzance which I always feel is more of a city station than a purely seaside one like Kingswear or St Ives. You will recall I have already shown a plan of this which was fairly accurate (plan 3.7), but when one has less space and one still needs a busy terminus to justify the train movements one wants to see, what is one to do?

Plan 6.7 is much more heavily compressed and the pointwork has been entirely redrawn to suit available RTR curved points. I have cheated in using the pre-1914 loco depot at the station rather than the later one at Long Rock but you can always miss out the shed if you want. In practical terms it has plenty enough track left to keep you busy and will take 6- or 7-coach trains depending on coach length. Now I have actually built this in my shed, so I know it works in practice. But would you be happy building this yourself, knowing how many compromises and distortions have been included? Would you re-name the station as a fictitious place and invent a new history? Or would you just model another station instead?

That is for you to say, but given the requirements one often has a basic choice between modelling something inaccurately that is ideal, or something less suitable

Plan 6.7
Penzuncle

1 Train shed
2 terraced houses on backscene
3 Roads
4 Goods shed
5 Platforms
6 Water tower
7 Coal
8 Turntable
9 Granite block sea wall and rocks
10 Signalbox
11 Engine shed

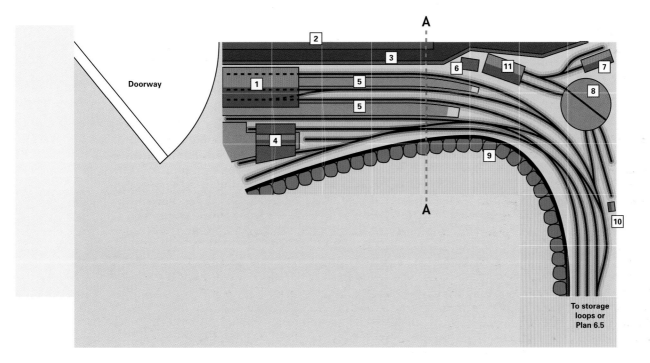

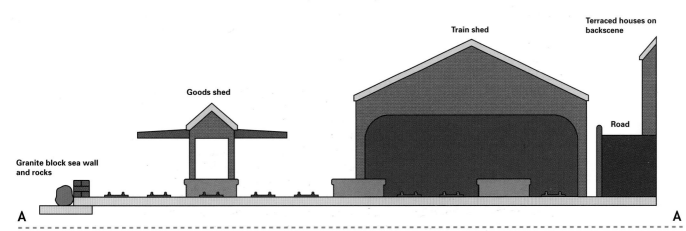

more accurately! Once again a compromise of some kind is necessary and it is for you to choose it. For me, I feel the station is still sufficiently recognisable as Penzance to be worthy of the name, and as I am particularly interested in operating the train services that ran to the station rather than creating a museum-standard model of it, it is much easier to run a believable Penzance-Paddington express train if you model Penzance than some fictitious terminus!

Another decision you will need to make when planning a layout is the proportion of town to countryside in your scenery. For example if one wants to cram the maximum amount of station operation into a shed, then a complete layout could be constructed from the plans of Truro and Charlotte Street in this chapter, which would stand intensive operation by three people when available. Or Penzance and Dawlish could be put together for a more rural scene while still maintaining main line operation.

I know many modellers like to model large amounts of grassy hillsides on their layout, and I often wonder about this. Does this really belong to the area modelled? In my experience it rarely does, as even when a real station is chosen, there is seldom much attempt to portray accurately the hillsides around the place. So do the grassy hillsides represent a deep-seated psychological need to show the countryside we all remember passing through on our railway journeys, or is it simply that the easiest way to fill an empty space is just to stick some netting and newspaper over it and paint it green?

Back to the City

We all need some 'scenery' to fill the bits of bare baseboard and show the division between railway and non-railway ground. But perhaps the scenery doesn't always need to be open countryside.

As one brought up in a busy city I like a layout to show the maze of tracks and sidings typical of a steam-age inner-city layout, as in plan 6.8. The hillsides

Plan 6.8

Hill Street

1 Warehouse
2 Large factory
3 Offices
4 Signalbox
5 Road
6 Houses
7 Privately owned
   yard
8 Beach
9 Terraced houses
10 Georgian
   terrace
11 Backscene
12 Window
13 Door

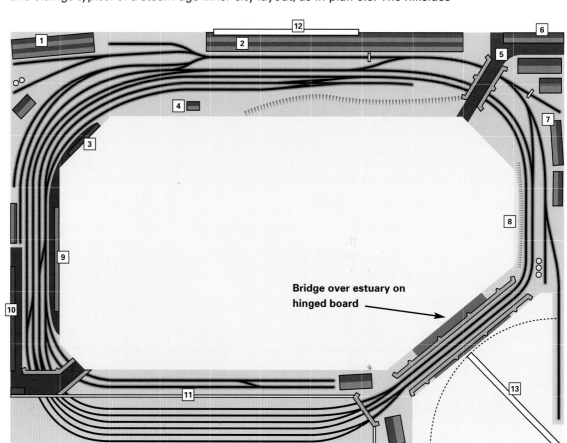

Bridge over estuary on hinged board

and backscenes are covered by houses and factory buildings which hide the railway in places, but reveal various private sidings and goods loops. In steam days all such businesses would have taken raw materials in and completed products out by rail, probably in covered vans, plus regular coal deliveries, so many freight trains could stop in the loops and shunt the sidings. Today rail-connected businesses are fewer and more specialised but a pile of pipes or scrap metal will look fine.

Freight could be a major activity on this layout and marshalling loops are included on the main straight so that every freight train can be re-formed at some point in its travels, and some private industry sidings nearby. It is both possible and sensible for some of the layout's freight trains to spend much of their time stored in view in these sidings and loops, just disappearing for a while off scene when necessary.

To maximise use of the precious inner perimeter of the layout the small space in front of the hidden storage loops is used for railway scenery. This could easily be a static non-railway scene, such as a building frontage, but as it is possible to put tracks there I have done this. Remember that although the layout looks very cramped with tracks, it will look less so when built, with some hidden and others dwarfed by the vertical structures (buildings, bridges, etc) around them. And of course tracks often *were* very cramped in the steam-age railway scene. So in plan 6.8 I have suggested the narrow space in front of the hidden storage loops could be used for a dockside scene, but it could equally well be part of a power station or coal distributor – anything that gets regular train loads.

When you haven't much space you need to use it effectively and low-relief buildings should be used plentifully against a city backscene. Even if (like me) you can't paint a realistic hillside it is easy to build an interesting city scene such as the dead-end Georgian terrace which can fit in the left-hand side. A road overbridge disguises the entry to the storage loops, but this is also an access point for the short terrace next to it. The terrace could have a stone wall around it but etched railings would look much better, with the odd weed or buddleia growing through them. If the road is tarmacked it should have a pavement but if unadopted by the local council it could be bare earth or gravel.

The layout corners are very important places too – try to imagine a full scene to put in them, like 'Hill Road' in the corner. This uses several tricks to suggest a large city in a small corner space. A diagonal road overbridge disguises the curvature of the main line, and the road is continued out of sight into the corner of the room, hidden behind a shop to the right. Always use the verticals in small spaces: I suggest the road is raised into a hill for interest, with each house higher than the one before it. Only the shop the other side of the road is fully modelled – everything else is low-relief and made from card kits.

The factory in the backscene is the front of another card kit; many such factories don't have visible roofs so you can stick the card directly to the backscene and it's amazing what you can do in an inch or less! Cut the backscene off at the roofline and put 'sky paper' on the walls of the room half an inch behind to make them stand out. A few 3-D details like windowsills and drainpipes work wonders too.

Now I won't labour what will be very obvious to some readers but I'll lay my cards on the table. If you are interested in modelling the city railway scene and trying to give the impression of the busy workaday scene in what may be a restricted modelling space, then you will have to pack a lot into a small space. The practical limitations we face as modellers – train length, curve radii, point dimensions – lay down a minimum space for the railway part of the city which may be a very high proportion of the whole space available to us, and leave only a little for scenery; but whereas this causes lots of trouble in a country scene – where it is difficult to convey the space and emptiness of the prototype without relying on artificial visual breaks – in a city the opposite is the case. Cities are busy places, and very cramped. Space costs money, so every corner is filled.

In a city model it is both easy and very realistic to cram house backs or factory walls next to the railway fence, and with a little attention to detail the low-relief backscene can carry the visual space of several streets in just a couple of inches.

So in a smaller room, although I'd happily swap fully modelled buildings for low-relief ones where this hasn't been done already, I would be very reluctant to lose even an inch of the small space I have left for low-relief buildings and backscenes; I would rather take away sidings to suit and adjust the maximum train length accordingly. Many urban trains were actually quite short, and in a busy urban railway scene it is not only permissible to cram as many sidings into a small space as can fit, it is actually more realistic to do so!

In the right-hand corner of plan 6.8 I have avoided the temptation to put grassy fields and instead have left more buildings, with again a mix of fully 3-D and low-relief, but this time serving a set of railway sidings alongside the main line that can be shunted in several ways. The loop in front of the factory allows a freight train to stop here and its wagons to be shunted amongst the many sidings, or the loop can be treated as simply a lay-by for other trains to pass it. The operational variations are endless.

Plan 6.8 has of course one glaring omission – it has no station. Does this matter?

I would argue that it does not, as the layout provides plenty of operation for goods and freight trains, and it is quite realistic to stop passenger trains in view while they wait for their route to be cleared. But if you do want a station, where can you put it?

The space where a station could go is used for the hidden storage loops, which are an essential part of running a realistic sequence of trains through the scenic section of the layout. Now I have already discouraged the idea of the basic continuous run with a plain circuit around the room to a station, because there is nowhere for trains to go but back into the station again and one ends up with a glorified train set rather than a model railway.

But hold on – in plan 6.8 we justified storing some of the freight trains in view on the grounds that it was realistic and prototypical. So why not take the idea further still and put all the storage loops in view?

I always feel it a shame to spend so much money on track and points only to hide them away. If you disguise them as a busy city station you get the benefits of train storage and a busy station for no extra cost. Plan 6.9 shows the idea. The station in the plan is on a curve, as was fairly common in urban areas, and is comparatively simple because it is not really intended to be the main focus of the layout. It is essentially just a way of turning the necessary storage space into a more realistic piece of railway scenery.

Train engines can be coaled and watered in the small servicing depot in the corner behind the station and swapped regularly to make the trains visibly different. Trains leaving the bay run around the layout in view, then stop in one of the curved platforms under the train shed. The locomotive would be removed and a fresh one added to the other end using the crossovers provided, which then becomes a down express to run around again until arriving at journey's end.

Once again if one had more space then the station could be 'uncramped' a little, but I feel it important to show that a viable, operable and fairly believable station is possible in a small space. Although it may not be clear in the plan, it is intended that only the extreme ends of the storage loops are in view and the middle is hidden behind a backscene representing the station building. If you can make a large overall roof you can also hide the train from view when it is supposedly somewhere else, and later run it forward a foot or two to show it 'arriving'. It can then run around the layout and disappear again.

If you don't have room for long enough loops then don't worry – in the steam age trains spent a lot of time stationary in major stations having their locos changed, and perhaps adding or removing restaurant cars or having the coaching rakes strengthened or shortened. If you add in some carriage sidings and a loco depot on the far side of the layout you can duplicate this and change every train into a different one on the layout without needing a fiddle-yard.

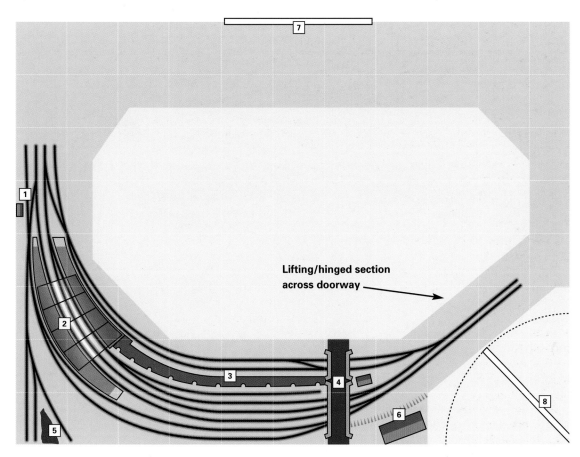

Lifting/hinged section
across doorway

Plan 6.9
Storage in view

1 Signalbox
2 Station
3 Retaining wall
4 Road
5 Coal
6 Hotel
7 Window
8 Door

Another option is to make the station bigger to store more trains, and to let it sprawl a little further around the room. This idea is taken further in the chapter on continuous-run layouts so I won't pursue it any further here. The plain fact of the matter is that if one wants to model a large city station – particularly a real one, in reasonable fidelity – it is very difficult to make an operable layout in a reasonable space if one sticks to the basic oval, unless one fills the rest of the space with storage loops. In some respects at least, it is much easier to make an out-and-back layout, and we will return to this for the remaining plans in this chapter.

Out-and-Back on the LNER

With its history of GNR Atlantics, 'A4' steam locomotives, 'Deltic' diesels, and then later Class 91 electrics, the ex-LNER main line has provided inspiration to generations of railway modellers, and the Mecca for many was King's Cross. But is it possible to make a respectable model of this in a normal room?

Or to re-phrase the question slightly, how much of the prototype can be included in such a room, in a model which is both believable and operable?

My answer is in plan 6.10. This attempts to fit as much of the station as possible into an 11ft x 8ft room and although it won't take 8-coach trains, it will handle six Gresley coaches and still leave enough space for other features like the loco servicing depot. There is even room for the ex-GNR goods depot and Top Shed in the corner. Obviously we can't model them fully, but we have to put the scenic boundary somewhere, and we can put it in the middle of the yard if it suits us! The shed itself is modelled in low relief to avoid cramping the depot and to allow the locomotives to be displayed – a trick worth remembering when you have to suggest a much bigger depot than you have room for.

'Bottom Shed' was used for locos that return home without visiting 'Top Shed', but also during peak times to hold locos out of the way before running up

Plan 6.10

Kings Cross

1   Coal
2   Bottom
    shed/offices
3   Turntable
4   Canal
5   Engine shed
6   Road
7   York Road
8   Signalbox
9   North down line
10 Offices
11 Goods shed
12 Goods sidings
13 Hinged bridge
14 Wall

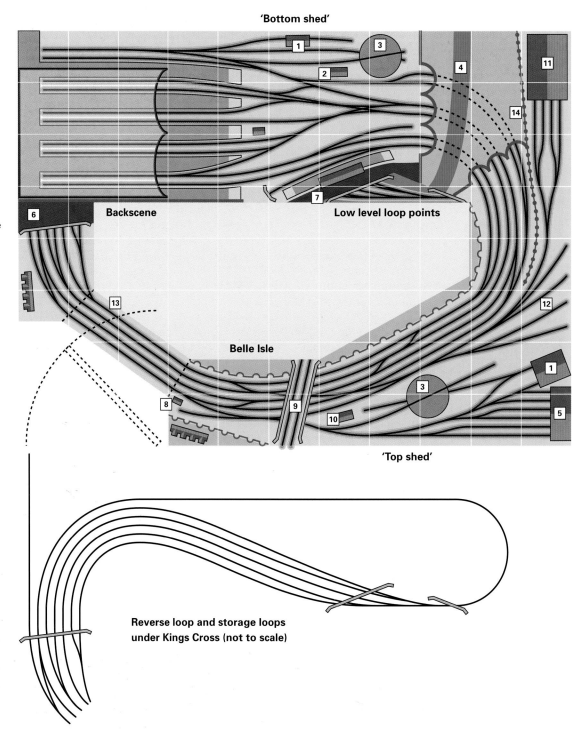

'Bottom shed'

Backscene

Low level loop points

Belle Isle

'Top shed'

**Reverse loop and storage loops
under Kings Cross (not to scale)**

to Top Shed. The four-track main line allows several trains to run at once which is great fun if you can stand the pace!

The low-level storage loops require the gradient to run the opposite way to real life but it should still be possible to make the Belle Isle scene quite realistic. The storage loops have been arranged so that all the points are easily accessible. Note that trains run around the reverse loop before entering the storage loops rather than afterwards, so that the inevitable wheel and flange friction helps slow the train down. If you start a long train from a loop and run it straight into a tight 200-degree bend before it has attained line speed there is no guarantee it will actually get through without a helping hand.

There is no doubt that the plan is a very tight fit in the 11ft x 8ft room drawn, and in a typical garage of approximately 14-16ft by 9-10ft it could be opened out nicely, with easier gradients and longer platforms, more non-railway scenery, and with much more room in the central area of the layout for the operators.

On the other hand, with this much space one could be a little more adventurous. Many modern houses have a single garage built in to them, and most of these seem to end up filled with bicycles, old kitchen units, inflatable boats and bits of motor vehicles. So why not use this space for a model railway as in the next plan? The layout will have to share the space but there is usually room to put it above the other items.

Now it is my lasting regret that I never visited the North of England in steam days, but if you did, or even lived there, you will no doubt remember the wonderful complexity of railway lines that grew out of the 19th century railway boom. Take Leeds, for example, where the Great Eastern, North Eastern, Lancashire & Yorkshire, London & North Western, and Midland Railways all had stations and goods depots (some of them jointly), and within a square mile or so could be found around six of each.

The centrepiece of this was arguably Leeds Central which (alas) disappeared at the end of steam but did see 'Deltics' in regular use. With 16ft available, plan 6.11 is my attempt to include as much of the real scene as is possible without excessive compression. It is just possible to include Leeds Central itself, three of the nearest goods depots, Copley Hill loco depot and even Holbeck high- and low-level stations. Fortunately the prototype itself was extremely cramped, and would no doubt have been rebuilt after the war if plans had not been afoot to rebuild the 'new' Leeds City station to the south.

Many long-distance passenger trains including a few named ones such as the 'Yorkshire Pullman' visited Leeds en route, reversing direction with a new loco on

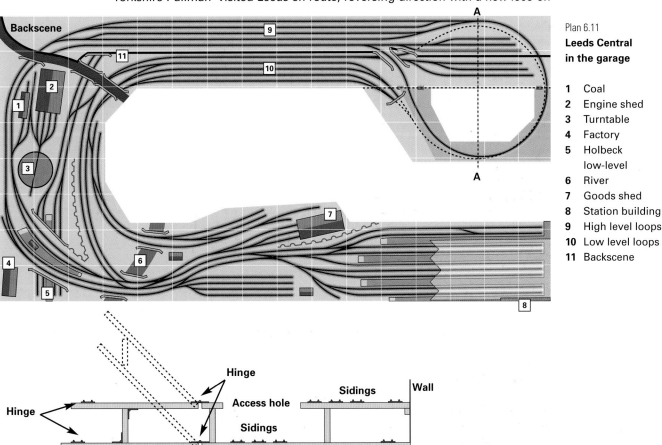

Plan 6.11
**Leeds Central
in the garage**

1   Coal
2   Engine shed
3   Turntable
4   Factory
5   Holbeck
    low-level
6   River
7   Goods shed
8   Station building
9   High level loops
10 Low level loops
11 Backscene

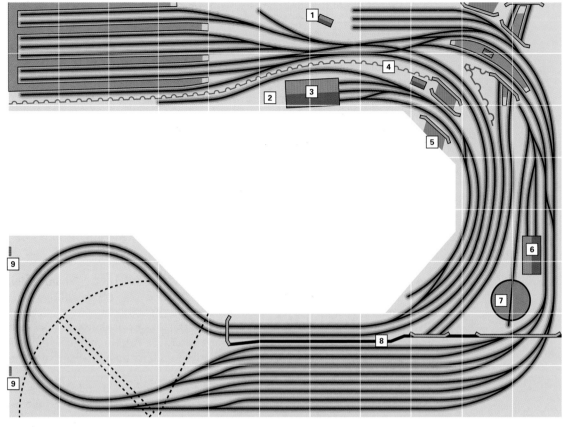

Plan 6.12

**Leeds Central
(reduced)**

1   Signalbox
2   Yard
3   Goods shed
4   Retaining wall
5   River
6   Engine shed
7   Turntable
8   Backscene
9   Hinges

the other end, so the layout design allows this to be modelled. Don't forget there were many local passenger trains for every long-distance express and local passenger trains can be run via Holbeck High Level station on the Bradford and Huddersfield line, and via Gerrard Junction on the lines to Harrogate and York.

The high-level LNWR/LYR joint goods depot had two distinctive square brick towers which housed wagon hoists; these allowed wagons to be dropped down to low-level goods yards on each side. There is just about room for one of these on the plan and it would make an interesting feature. Holbeck Low Level is suggested on the Midland lines below, and I have suggested that these can be operated independently as a shuttle between hidden sidings in the tunnels if desired or could be purely static. The layout itself is in the form of a 'Y' with a two separate out-and-back runs through hidden storage loops on two levels, each of which has its own reverse loop. Although there aren't many storage loops, the upper ones are long enough to store two trains end to end.

In practical terms the reverse loop takes up space near the garage door which will be needed for entry, so the layout section that sticks out there will need either to hinge out of the way or be removed bodily after operation finishes. The sketch shows how I would do this: the two levels of the layout are both hinged upward, the lower one having a hinged leg which drops down to the floor to support it. The upper board is held in place with a spacing piece that is hinged to both top and bottom boards and allows both boards to fold up together easily. A cutaway in the upper board provides hand access to the lower sidings.

Dead-end sidings are included to provide storage for DMUs and light locos that don't need to reverse. It is easy to forget how many light engine movements there were in steam days and these provide an easy means of increasing the variety of train movements without needing much extra storage. Locomotives can be swapped in the storage loops (not by hand, please!) with light locos sent out specially from the locomotive depot and the tired ones run back there. This kind of operational detail is often missed out but can make the difference between playing trains and running a railway.

Not that there's anything wrong with just playing trains – I like to do it myself! – but it is good to operate a layout like the real thing occasionally as well as make it look like the real thing. Which brings me onto a further point that I think needs stressing. A layout of this complexity will need a good deal of effort to build, and possibly more than one person can manage. But it will also need more than one person to operate it properly too. It is certainly possible to run it single-handed but for intensive operation the layout could easily occupy two people on platform duty with a further two on the main lines and storage loops and one each on the loco depot and goods yards. In reality the layout could be operated well with just two or three patient people who know it well and can multi-task, and a timetable would help enormously here.

However, with a little more compression Leeds Central can be fitted into an 11ft x 8ft room, and plan 6.12 is the result. In the smaller space there is insufficient room for the gradients of the prototype and the main lines form a simple out-and-back run through a single set of storage loops. Although this has some drawbacks from the strict perspective of route operation, it does allow a decent scenic run and is much easier to operate single-handed. In some ways I prefer it to the larger plan. The station is hardly changed but the high- and low-level goods depots have been merged; northbound goods trains can arrive in the station and be shunted down to the low-level goods depot as I think happened on the prototype.

Of course one difference between a garage space and a normal room is the position of the door. In the smaller plan I have suggested that the reverse loop hinges up to the end wall, the opposite to the usual arrangement. If this is non-scenic it can fold flat to the wall and occupy little space. This allows normal access to the room when operation is not under way and helps to keep the household authorities sweet!

My last city layout, plan 6.13, is set in Glasgow. The station at St Enoch formed the northern terminus of the Glasgow & South Western Railway, which operated in a triangle with Stranraer and Carlisle. It opened in 1876, merged with the LMS in 1924, and closed in 1966, as did the Caledonian's nearby Buchanan Street. St Enoch was sometimes referred to as Scotland's St Pancras and had several similarities including the gothic overall roof and the adjacent hotel which was once the largest in Scotland. This could make a nice backscene, whether in low relief or fully modelled, but the distinctive train shed is, as usual, inconvenient for manual operation unless removed. This time I suggest it is regarded as a scenic dust-cover! The distinctive signal bridge (gantry) was one of the largest in the world with 66 signal arms.

The end of an era at Glasgow St Enoch as Standard class tank 80054 pulls out of Glasgow St Enoch in 1966 on a relief to Ayr. The curved points and slips are characteristic but difficult to replicate with RTR pointwork unless simplified. (Photo Derek Cross)

Plan 6.13

Glasgow St Enoch

1   Overall roof
2   Passenger
    subway
3   Parcels subway
4   Water tower
5   Signalbox
6   Coal stage
7   Turntable
8   Engine shed
9   Goods shed
10 Signal gantry
11 Road
12 River

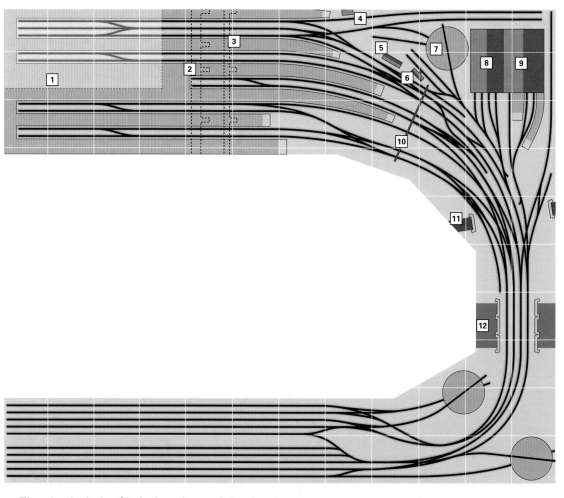

The plan includes Clyde Junction and the river bridge, and just enough of the other two arms of the triangle to Saltmarket Junction to store DMUs out of view if desired. In the middle of this triangle lay a large shed which, rather unusually, had a four-road locomotive shed on one side and a three-road goods shed for fish, fruit and milk on the other.

With twelve platforms the station is too large to model exactly, so I have reduced the number by two without, I hope, losing much of the character, and it could lose another two without becoming too silly. It's worth commenting here that even if you had plenty of space and money, it would still (in my opinion) be a mistake to try to model St Enoch exactly since it would be almost impossible to run sufficiently intensive train services without a huge number of operators. For the same reason the complex pointwork of the original (which was intended to allow very many simultaneous train and locomotive movements) would be quite impossible to operate reliably and prototypically without an interlocking system like the prototype, and so this has also been simplified greatly. However, I have kept the distinctive dead ends between the tracks that were used to hold locomotives and which, between them, accessed all platforms.

I've always been fascinated by large city stations and have often attempted to model them in spaces not *quite* large enough for the purpose, usually by simplifying them greatly. However the prevailing modelling style today is to make an 'exact' model which - if taken literally - simply prevents one modelling these at all. I feel this is a shame, but if you want to try your hand at building plans like those in this chapter it leads to a manor problem - how much do you simplify the plan?

In the plans of King's Cross, Glasgow St Enoch and Leeds Central I am guilty of reducing the number of platforms and simplifying the station throats. But have I simplified them enough? In each case I have tried to preserve the spirit of the trackwork rather than the letter, but in each case what results is *still* highly complex, and DCC (digital command control) would be almost essential.

Although I generally try to work out accurately how the track plan can be implemented with ready-to-run points, in very complex curved throats like this it is difficult to be sure whether they will fit in as planned without actually laying them out full size. More than once I have had to revise substantially my intended station pointwork to make it fit properly and work well (and indeed to be 'wire-upable' without nightmares). So if you're building anything like this, make sure you lay out some of the trackwork before you cut the baseboards to size!

Anyone attempting to build plans as complex as these should appreciate the size of the task they are attempting, and that this will probably need more than two hands to build. Frankly, they would suit a club layout more tha a home layout and in this case it may be possible to increase the baseboard size and uncramp them a little. In most of these plans I have consciously compressed them to the maximum extent possible on the basis that it is easier for the reader to expand them again to fit a slightly larger room.

Although this book was written chiefly for the modeller in '00' gauge (4mm scale), the super-detailed models now available ready-to-run in 'N' gauge (2mm scale) make this a solution to many of the difficulties discussed above. now it is often stated that a 2mm scale plan will need only half the length and a quarter of the area of a 4mm scale plan, but if the 4mm plan has been compressed heavily it may make more sense to keep the 2mm scale model the same physical size and just to spread the tracks out a little. I feel this is particularly true for city stations where the inevitable reduction in platform width that is necessary in 4mm scale seems to be much more noticeable in 2mm scale. The other benefit of changing to 2mm scale in the same physical space is the possibility of running scale-length trains.

St Enoch is intended to be operated fairly prototypically. It is designed for intensive operation and can easily occupy four people (two on the station, one on the locomotive and goods shed, and one in the fiddle-yard). The key to implementing the high train frequency of the prototype successfully will certainly be the fiddle-yard. There are a great many types of these but the vast majority are not ideal for main line layouts because they are too slow to operate. The one shown here is unusual with its two turntables but is really two separate yards that are designed for rapid turnaround on a four-track main line. Club layouts would probably use hand-built scissors crossings here but the commercial double-slips I have drawn should be quite adequate.

Every time a train arrives at the fiddle-yard it stops with the rear coupling of the engine over an uncoupling ramp, and a new locomotive immediately backs onto the train from the turntable. Every train in the fiddle-yard therefore has a loco at both ends, which means that the layout can easily absorb two dozen locomotives and more without a large loco depot or even locos spurs in the fiddle-yard.

Whenever a train leaves the fiddle-yard the original train engine follows it out (as it would do in a real station) and the double-slip is switched to let the locomotive run straight onto the turntable to be turned, ready for the next train, and leaving the siding empty again. The central siding can be used to hold spare coaches, restaurant cars, parcel vans and horseboxes for attachment to and detachment from occasional trains to vary their appearance, and this again is a simple and quick process.

You will note that practical operation of the fiddle-yard is very close indeed to that of the station itself, which is no coincidence at all! So I would be strongly tempted to make the fiddle-yard itself scenically into a station, perhaps by deleting one of the turntables and adding a goods depot there, so that both operators get a taste of real station operation. Of course very many other out-and-back layout designs are possible, many of which could be a good deal simpler than those presented here. But I hope these plans show that it is possible to build and operate a realistic model of a major city station, and give some idea how this can be done in a reasonable space.

CHAPTER

The Goods Yard

Along with the loco shed which we looked at in an earlier chapter, the goods yard is possibly one of the most frequently misunderstood and poorly modelled adjuncts to the steam-age railway. A major reason for this could be that most of us never had the chance to stay around and see the yards in operation, usually just passing through on trains, gaining a brief snapshot of wagons and vans ideal in sidings and loops, or perhaps being shunted by a small tank engine or diesel shunter.

Of course there are plenty of more-or-less accurate track plans available of real stations which we can examine and even copy but the majority are much too large to copy exactly and too complex to understand clearly, so in simplifying them it is difficult to make sure we have still maintained a workable goods yard.

Does that matter?

I think it does, because it seems ironic to me how many modellers who can expound in tedious detail all the errors of the latest super-detailed model from Hornby or Bachmann are nevertheless quite incapable of planning or building a goods yard that is remotely realistic, or appreciating why their effort is not. Lest this sound too harsh a criticism, let me say at once that for most of my modelling career I undoubtedly fell into the same group, so I know fairly well the depth of my own previous ignorance!

In the steam age most stations had a goods yard of some kind even if it was a single siding, and I'm sure most of us have at some time just stuck a couple of sidings on one side and called it a goods yard. After all, this is what the railway companies did, more or less, isn't it?

To some extent they did, but they did have some rules and if you aren't careful it is all too easy to end up with something that is untypical and unrealistic such as plan 7.1a. How many things can you see wrong with this?

Well, to start with there's a facing point on the up main line which the railway companies – and the Board of Trade which governed them – disliked intensely. If the yard had to be in a facing position it would probably have trailed into the

Before the mechanical horse and then the lorry took over, the real horse was the mainstay of goods traffic on its journey from the railway yard to the shop or business. In this pre-war scene at an unidentified LMS yard note how the wicker baskets and cardboard boxes were stacked at an angle on the carts. (Ian Allan Library)

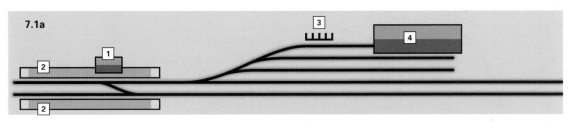

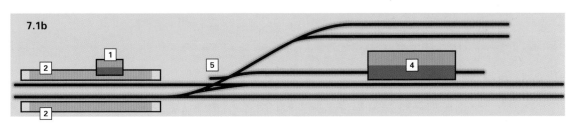

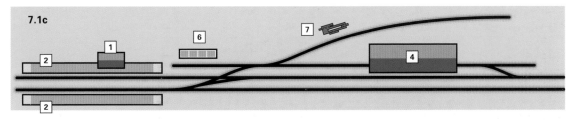

Plan 7.1a,b,c.

Bad goods yards

1   Station Building
2   Platforms
3   Coal bins
4   Goods shed
5   Trap point
6   Cattle dock
7   Crane

down line as shown in plan 7.1b, perhaps with a single-slip (but not a double) for use as a main line crossover, and would probably be clear of the up platform.

Then there's the goods shed. Although goods sheds were sometimes stuck on the ends of sidings, this made them much more time-consuming to shunt so they were usually placed in the middle of the siding as in plan 7.1b, or on a loop so that a rake of wagons and vans could be pushed along to give each one a turn in the shed. And remember, if you shunt covered vans into a goods yard, you will need to shunt them to the shed at some point to be unloaded, not just let them sit around forgotten!

Another snag is the poor access to the two sidings nearest the main lines, with nowhere to park a cart and the main line so close it would be hazardous to unload anything from them. The arrangement in plan 7.1b is much better. If you haven't much space then it is better to miss out one of the sidings entirely as in plan 7.1c and leave the space between tracks. A small hand crane would be useful too.

A further problem with the first plan is that the yard can only be shunted easily by down trains, and the addition of points trailing into the up line in plan 7.1c allows up trains to drop off vans and wagons in the goods shed as well. Wagons needed elsewhere could be moved around the yard by hand with a pinch bar or by horse. The horse was widely used for this, which explains why some real station yards look like they can't be shunted properly with an engine (eg those curious wooden turntables you see in early plans). Steam locomotives were often banned from running through goods sheds, though there is photographic evidence that they did run through when needed, so don't worry too much if your shed can't be worked any other way!

Another flaw in plan 7.1a is the lack of any trap points to derail wayward wagons before they strayed onto the main line. Every yard or siding joining a main line would certainly have either trap points as in plan 7.1b, or a headshunt, tailshunt or siding as in plan 1c, where the points, even if hand-operated by a ground frame nearby, would be interlocked with the main line and signals to prevent accidents.

The coal bins in plan 7.1a are also not ideal. They back up against the track, a common feature of model layouts but much rarer on the real railway and very unlikely to be found next to the goods shed since goods and coal were distinct

Plan 7.2

Langport West (GWR)

1   Station Building
2   Platforms
3   Footbridge
4   Cattle dock
5   Waiting Room
6   Trap point
7   Loading Dock
8   Goods shed
9   Office

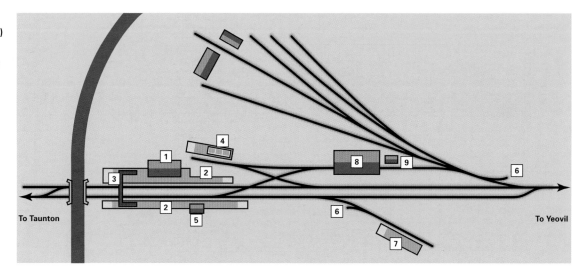

Plan 7.3

Badmington (GWR)

1   Station Building
2   Platforms
3   Footbridge
4   Waiting Room
5   Goods shed
6   Cattle pens
7   Signalbox
8   Offices
9   Loading dock
LG Loading gauge

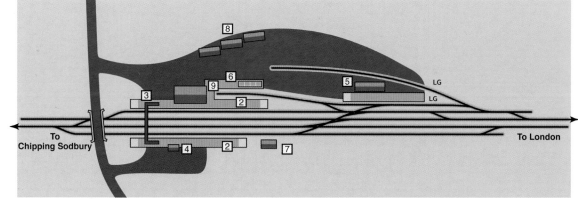

Plan 7.4

St Annes-on-the-sea (LMS)

1   Platforms
2   Crane
3   Goods shed
4   Cattle shed
5   Stables
6   Signalbox
7   Gate
8   Fence

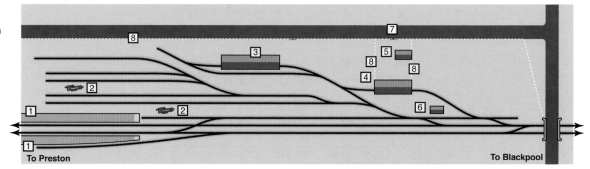

traffic. Many small railway yards didn't use bins at all, and those that did generally placed them away from the tracks. On the other hand almost every goods yard had cattle pens, so plan 7.1c has a new spur for cattle pens and the coal bins have been removed.

Plans 7.2, 7.3, and 7.4 show some real station yards for comparison. Langport West (plan 7.2) is a generic type of small yard favoured by the GWR which could easily be extended to a four-track main line as in Badminton (plan 7.3). Chipping Sodbury was almost identical though plans show an extra siding with a loading platform. However, sidings tended to get added and taken away at frequent intervals throughout their lives, so I wouldn't take any published plans as exact without a dated photograph. In both of these plans you will notice the additional trailing crossover to the cattle bay.

You may note the lack of headshunts in plans 7.2 to 7.4; some railway companies (like the Midland) used them widely, whereas others like the GWR seemed to use them hardly at all. So if you are modelling a particular location it is worth checking the stations in that area to see what the 'house style' was for the company that made them.

Anyway, having had a quick look at what can go wrong with even a simple goods yard plan, let's look at the various goods traffic in more detail.

Coal Traffic

In the early years of the railway every house and every industry used coal, and the only practical means of delivery was the railway until cheap war-surplus lorries arrived in 1920 and again in 1945.

In the NE Region the stationmaster was often also the coal agent and would order coal to be delivered to the station where it could be dropped through doors in the bottom of the wagon and holes in the track to a set of bins below, often covered by stone buildings, from where it could be sold to customers by the agent.

If you want to model this yourself, good examples are to be seen at Beamish museum in Yorkshire and at Goathland station on the NYMR. The LNER consequently had a large fleet of its own hopper wagons for the purpose at a time when most other railway companies owned hardly any company coal wagons except those used for their own consumption (eg locomotive coal).

However, coal drops like this were pretty uncommon in other regions where the railway company's interest stopped when the wagon had been delivered to the yard. Before nationalisation in 1948, most coal was carried on the railway in wooden-planked wagons privately owned by either the colliery or the trader, and unloading it in the yard would be the responsibility of the local coal merchant. He would be allowed a few days to unload the wagon and if the wagon wasn't emptied and moved on after that he would be charged 'demurrage' for occupying the company's rails.

The merchant would want to transfer the coal out of the wagon as quickly as possible, preferably straight into hundredweight sacks (112lb, about 50kg) for delivery to people's homes. The easiest way for him to do that would be to shovel the coal out of the wagon into bags suspended from a hook attached to a weighing machine on his (horse-drawn) cart. When the bag was filled it would be put on the cart and the next bag filled. When the cart was full any remaining

This wonderfully evocative scene at Leeds Central low-level yard is undated but is full of period detail and clutter for the post-war period. The ex-NER warehouse and yard is on the left and the GNR warehouse is right of centre. Note the huge pile of timber and the Scammell mechanical horses parked in front. (Ian Allan Library)

Plan 7.5

Bicester (LMS)

1   Station building
2   Waiting Room
3   Goods shed
4   Cattle dock
5   Stable
6   Office
7   Signalbox
8   Horse landing
9   Gate
10 Coal stacking area, with small huts
11 Small Crane
12 Loading gauge
13 Trap points
14 Ground frame
15 **Dock**

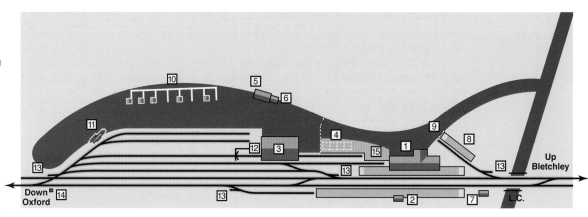

bags could be left on the ground for collection later. Many yards had just a coal stacking ground between sidings for this purpose, where heaps of coal or filled bags of coal could be deposited.

What the merchant wouldn't want to do would be to drop all the coal in the wagon directly into bins or wharves (not staithes – this term is more properly used for those large elevated tracks that ran to docks to load coal into ships) as this would involve lots of extra manual labour lifting it out again into bags; since the yards were open to the public he might also have trouble with coal disappearing.

The exception was large coal yards where there wouldn't be enough labour to bag all the coal up immediately, and here bins were often provided, often many feet from the tracks, either in the middle of the yard or against a boundary fence as in Bicester (LMS), in plan 7.5. Where coal traffic was heavy there might be several coal merchants operating in the yard and the bins would be labelled with the owner's name. At Bicester some of the larger bins had small huts in them for the merchants.

Manufacturing industries also used coal and a factory that was rail-connected for import of raw materials or export of finished goods could also have a coal bin or even a separate coal siding near to the boiler room. These

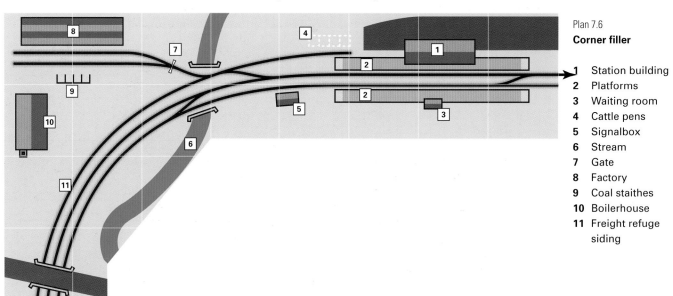

Plan 7.6

Corner filler

1   Station building
2   Platforms
3   Waiting room
4   Cattle pens
5   Signalbox
6   Stream
7   Gate
8   Factory
9   Coal staithes
10 Boilerhouse
11 Freight refuge siding

kinds of facilities are seldom modelled but plan 7.6 shows a corner on a freelance layout can be usefully filled.

There are a great variety of private-owner coal wagons available for the modeller today and these can look very pretty with their bright colours, but we should remember that by BR days most of them would be very old, dirty, and either broken or recently repaired. In fact after nationalisation BR had so much trouble with these old wagons that they were soon replaced by steel wagons owned by BR. Virtually all the old wagons had gone by the late 1950s, but coal merchants were also gradually transforming from small one-man operations to larger firms with their own private coal yards and fleets of ex-army petrol and diesel lorries. They took delivery of whole rakes of wagons and (by the 1960s) started to use mechanised handling equipment such as conveyor belts. Most of the old bins dropped out of use then.

A series of extremely unpleasant smogs in major cities after World War 2 also led to the clean air acts that gradually forced most city dwellers to forsake coal for smokeless fuels like coke. By 1960 many houses had also changed to central heating with a commercial boiler using coke-based fuels such as anthracite, usually in specialised grades and sizes of pellet to feed properly into the boiler, and these couldn't be provided by the traditional coal man from the station yard. The rise in labour costs and cheaper lorry transport which made large central depots more economic helped to end the life of the traditional local coal yard. Today of course gas and electricity are the main power sources of domestic heating.

Livestock

The other specialised traffic that the steam-age goods yard had to accommodate was livestock. Cattle and sheep were bred in country areas and usually taken to market in a large town. So every station on a line through countryside where cattle or sheep grazed would have a siding somewhere with a platform adjacent for this traffic to be loaded, and with fenced pens to hold them. Cattle are messy creatures and the platform and track would need to be hosed down after use; many cattle docks therefore had the rails of the adjacent track laid in concrete so that they could be washed clean after use – something else seldom modelled!

A large town with a livestock market might see dozens of sheep or cattle arrive on one day. A lot of pens would be needed side by side to hold the livestock from a rake of trucks, and these would have to be shunted around the yard in groups to give each a turn at the pens. The empties would also be stored. The market would probably be quite close to the railway and could make an interesting modelling scene. Plan 7.4 shows a compacted version of St Anne's on Sea (LMS) which had a large cattle dock on a loop and would suit a long narrow space.

Horses on the other hand were valuable creatures and usually carried singly or in pairs in a special horsebox attached to passenger trains, though when empty the vans could be taken by loose-coupled goods trains. Horseboxes would have accommodation for the groom and would generally be left at a passenger bay, though some stations had a very short end-loading bay which was dedicated to horses and horse-carriages, the latter carried in a carriage truck. A gentleman on a long journey might take both a carriage and horses with him.

At Bicester (plan 7.5) there was a long 'horse landing' platform on its own siding on the up side, installed for use by gentlemen visiting the local hunt. Despite its comparatively small size Bicester is an interesting plan in several respects, for example the double end-bay with no passenger access and the curious short down siding. This siding also had no platform bay and no road access either; it was much too short as a refuge for slow freights, so what was its purpose? My guess is that it was for horseboxes, to be dropped from or picked up by down passenger trains conveniently without delaying the service. The crossover halfway down the platforms would no doubt help here.

The Goods Shed

In steam days there were essentially three different ways to carry goods by rail. If you had enough of it you could book an open wagon or closed van (or supply your own) in which case the railway company would undertake to deliver it to the yard at the station specified and would notify you of its arrival. In this case, as with coal, its responsibility usually ended there and you would be expected to come to the yard to collect it in your own time. Long open platforms were often provided for this, where stone or hay or bags of fertiliser or cement etc could be off-loaded by hand and loaded (also by hand) onto the owner's cart.

Where a platform wasn't provided there were usually long sidings in the yard where the wagons would be left for unloading. You should note that these tracks were commonly arranged in pairs as in plan 7.4, so that one side of each wagon was easily accessed from a cartway. As loads of this kind were charged for mileage only, these were sometimes known as 'mileage' sidings.

The other option was to convey a load as either goods or parcels. The distinction between these two isn't always obvious, but in principle parcels were conveyed between stations in the guard's van of a passenger train and secured in the parcels office. This was expensive but fast and secure. Large city stations would often have bays dedicated to this traffic, or even a separate parcels depot like that at Paddington.

Less urgent small loads would be consigned between goods depots and would be loaded by the railway company onto open wagons or in closed vans in the depot. The route and timing of these loads was much less certain than parcels, and the wagons and vans could make many separate journeys (mostly short 'trip' workings) between different yards before they arrived at their intended destination. On arrival they would be unloaded by the railway company at a goods shed and stored there until collected.

At small stations most traffic was carried by the 'pick-up goods' which ran from station to station, stopping at each. The goods train would usually stop on the main line and the guard would screw down the handbrake. The locomotive and the front few wagons would be uncoupled and the wagons shunted into or out of the siding or goods shed and the train re-formed. The guard would check the couplings and then release his brake.

However, many station yards had other traffic of less obvious kinds, and these can make an interesting variation for a model. The LSWR station at Crediton, for example (plan 7.7) had a manure store and a slaughterhouse adjacent to one track, and a cider store on another. Like most other stations, it had both up and down sidings and a bewildering variety of stores and office buildings dotted around the yard.

Plan 7.7

Crediton

1   Station building
2   Platform
3   Waiting room
4   Loading dock
5   Goods shed
6   Store
7   Stable
8   Cattle pen
9   Signalbox
10 Coal staithe
11 Crane
12 Sheds
13 Manure store
14 Slaughter house
15 Cider store
16 Ground frame
17 Stream
LG Loading gauge

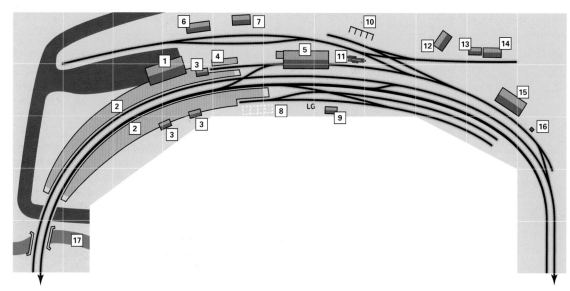

Having said earlier that most sidings were carefully arranged to give maximum practical access and plenty of standing ground adjacent, there were exceptions! The main one was for yards used to store rakes of wagons in transit, usually to allow them to be re-sorted into different trains. These could be closely spaced with no public access, and were common in large cities and near main line junctions. There were also much larger marshalling yards used for this purpose, and also various types of specialised yard for particular traffic (eg timber).

Following the Prototype

Although in many places in this book I urge readers to follow the prototype, there are dangers in doing this too!

The first point to make is that a great many of the goods yards attached to small railway stations were designed to a common pattern, as we saw earlier in the GWR examples. This is great for modelling but gets a little boring, particularly when they are so well laid out that operating them is too easy. Occasionally a deliberate snarl-up can be designed in to generate some creative solutions to shunting problems. One favourite device is the kickback siding, which typically trails off the loop in the opposite direction to all the other sidings and therefore needs extra shunting operations to use.

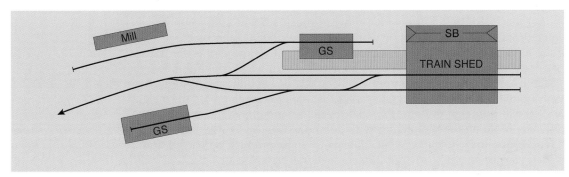

Plan 7.7a
Ashburton (original)

A well-known example of this is the GWR terminus at Ashburton in Devon, on the branch from Totnes (plan 7.7a). This prototype was a very popular choice for branch-line modellers some years ago, though it has several untypical and unwelcome features. For example the short train shed is very cute but by the postwar period very few examples of this GWR eccentricity remained and these are pretty well known, so it may not be a good idea to put this on a freelance station. Secondly the engine shed, which was so much a part of the GWR branch-line scene, serves very little actual purpose on the model and indeed on most such branches these became disused by the start of the grouping period in 1924.

But the biggest problem with the layout is the kickback siding. The siding can only be accessed from the bay, which means the bay has to be empty. If there is something in the bay, tough luck. You'll have to move it! Secondly, as the locomotive will be on the wrong end of the wagon or rake of wagons (not that you can use a long rake) you will have to run round it. There happens to be a convenient loop for the purpose, so what's the problem?

If the station is nearly empty there isn't a problem. But if there is a large collection of vans and wagons, where do they go? We have already seen the bay can't be used. Some of them could be put on the main line (which was frowned upon for obvious reasons) or else they will need to be shunted around the loop as well. And what if the locomotive required to do the shunting came up on a local passenger train? Or the commonplace mixed passenger/goods train? Where do the coaches go?

At this point you may, in exasperation, ask how the prototype was operated – which is a very good question and deserves some study. There were essentially four ways an awkward siding could or would have been operated in this or other stations. Two of these were often officially frowned upon and sometimes even banned by direct order from head office but still took place on occasion. These were fly shunting and use of a rope.

In the basic form of fly shunting a locomotive would push a wagon at speed along the track and then brake heavily, relying on a shunter to switch the point blades to allow the wagon to run or 'fly' into a siding while the locomotive carried straight on the main line. The other version which was often necessary but rather more hazardous was to pull the wagon along the track at speed, and (following release of the coupling by a shunter sat on the loco's buffer beam) the locomotive would accelerate sharply while a third man would fling the point blades over to allow the wagon to fly into the kickback siding.

The dangers in this practice, both to the workforce and to the vehicles, are obvious. It is interesting in these litigious days that this practice was carried on against management orders rather than because of them. The rope method was slightly safer but not always reliable. In this a locomotive on one track would pull a wagon on a parallel or diverging track along by means of a rope between the buffers of the two vehicles.

The third method, which was usually legal and comparatively safe, was to use a pinch bar. This was a long pole with an angled end which could be placed on the rail under the wheel of a wagon and could lever the wagon slowly along the track. However, it was very slow and also quite hard work. Fine to move a wagon a few feet, perhaps, but you wouldn't want to move it very far, very often.

But the main method by which most of these smaller station yards were worked, and were designed to be worked form their outset, was by horse. It was quite easy to get the horse to move one wagon at a time along the track as required, into or out of the goods shed and to or from the coal or cattle pens. The horse would also have no trouble pulling wagons at right angles to the main track from those small wooden turntables that are often seen on old track plans.

You will note that the one thing all these methods have in common is the difficulty in doing them realistically on a model. So, not for the first time, we have to face the choice between operating an accurately portrayed station inaccurately or operating an inaccurate or fictional station realistically.

I would therefore prefer the altered layout of 7.7b over the original in 7.7a, as the kickback siding is run off the platform loop instead which makes operation much less awkward. The single slip also gives a short run-round that works even while the platform is occupied (with coaches or a train being formed), and the up end of the loop is moved further along the main line as well. Finally the old engine shed – which served no useful purpose – has been deleted and a new siding with a crane added instead to hold all the wagons and vans that won't go anywhere else.

Plan 7.7b
Ashburton (modified)

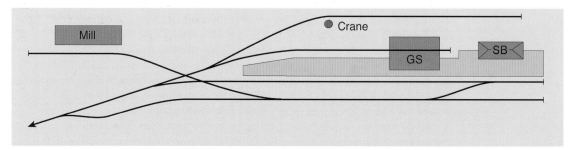

Now if you have accepted the need to change the track plan, you will already have realised the need to change the name of the station to something fictional. This is an excellent idea, as it allows one to follow as much of the prototype as one can or will do, while excusing any changes that one makes for whatever reason. But if you prefer to model a real station on the GWR network there are plenty of other to choose from and I would pick just two, Marlow and Calne, to demonstrate the goods facilities.

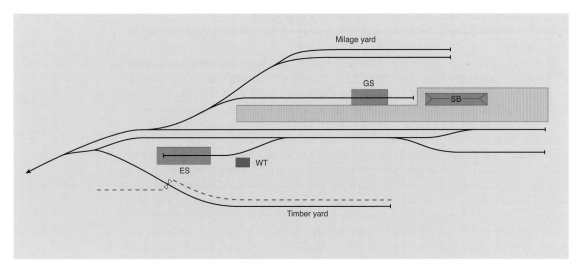

Plan 7.8
Marlow (simplified)
[not to scale –
diagrammatic only]

Marlow (which I have simplified slightly for plan 7.8) has much in common with the amended plan of Ashburton, except that the engine shed is still present and in place of the kickback private siding there is a normal one to a timber yard on the opposite side of the line. Calne (again simplified slightly for plan 7.9) is rather bigger than Ashburton but contains useful facilities including a milk dock, a large loading platform and a private siding for Harris's sausage plant, adjacent to the covered platform. The sidings beyond the gate were apparently used for coal and salt.

You will note that putting all the sidings on the near side of the station leaves space for a much longer platform. This could occasionally be useful, eg for troop trains serving a nearby military camp. As the layout develops over time it is easy to add a bay behind the station (shown dotted) and to imagine the town has grown in size to use more and heavier daily passenger traffic in addition to the mid-morning and mid-afternoon auto-train shuttle, and this complements the goods activities there.

I would certainly recommend using or inventing a station which did have a distinct amount of specialised goods traffic in addition to the usual coal and cattle, as without it station operation can be a little dull. Many small stations saw very few trains each day and those were pretty similar to one another. Even to the ardent railway modeller, one cattle wagon looks like another and one coal truck does too. This will leave both the operator and the viewing audience (if any) deeply bored and very quickly. What usually happens is that the builder, finding the model complete and also rather dull to operate even at exhibitions, puts it up for sale after a short time or dismantles it to build something else. Now if this is your own aim, don't let me stop you, but I do feel there are a lot of alternatives which are better!

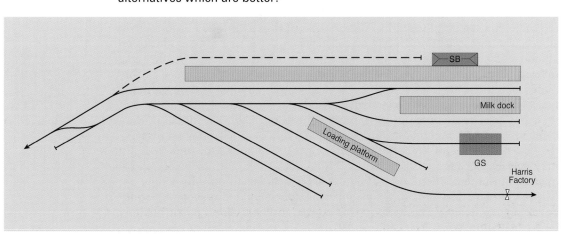

Plan 7.9
Calne (simplified)
[dotted line is
possible bay
addition]

Modelling the Prototype

Although many of us can trace our interest in railway modelling to an early train set as a child, I suspect that most of us were probably attracted to it by its relationship with the real railway and our interaction with it either in daily travel or holiday excursions, or standing by the lineside watching trains go by.

It follows, therefore, that as railway modellers we are not content merely to play with the toys that run along on wheels, but we need, somehow, to relate our modelling efforts to the real thing – the real railway. There are many ways to do that and I have tried to illustrate several of them in this book. Some of us like to capture the essence of a great many scenes and memories in a freelance model layout; some of us like to re-create the operational aspects of the real railway, working to timetable; others are never happier than when we are just watching the trains go by. Some modellers like to aim for the most exact portrayal of a single railway scene that it is possible to achieve, and even if it is an imaginary location the attention to detail and authenticity which is created can be wonderful. I know some modellers who think of this as modelling without compromise and a few who are dismissive of anything which does not at least have this as its aim.

But compromise there still is. The scene portrayed is a tiny one – just a few hundred yards, perhaps – and on it trains appear like actors on a stage, spouting their lines to disappear a moment later. The other side of the backscene may be a fiddle-yard, which represents the backstage area of the theatre and on which the stage hands do the horribly unprototypical things needed to ensure the show goes on. Or perhaps we eschew the fiddle-yard and use instead a set of hidden storage loops. This is better in some respects but compromise is still involved, in that the trains really do run around in circles even if this is cleverly disguised. But we still have the choice between making an exact model of a small part of the scene that interests us or compressing reality to fit the entire scene into the space available.

Perhaps the least compromise is required in a terminal station operated with hidden reverse loops, though in reality the trains still disappear off-scene quickly after leaving the station. But I can't help feeling that in all these kinds of layout there is still something missing. To put it in a nutshell, we are all supposed to be railway modellers, but how many of us really try to model a railway as such? Most of us are content to model only a very small piece of a railway – often less than a mile in scale terms. But it wasn't always like this.

Fifty years ago many layouts were designed as 'system' layouts to provide exciting operation for a band of enthusiasts. These layouts always had at least two main stations – usually more – and the whole point of them was to allow operators in different stations to despatch and receive trains in a prototypical manner, usually to a timetable.

In those days the scenery was often poor or non-existent, and the quality of the individual locomotives and rolling stock was also variable. Frequently a station with three platforms might be called King's Cross or Paddington with no embarrassment whatever. But that didn't matter because the aim was to *run* a railway, not to stand back and criticise it. Railway modelling was a social activity rather than the solitary pursuit of scenic modelling it so often is today, and the typical club layout would be operated intensively at each club night.

It is a continual source of disappointment to me how few model railway clubs today use club nights for proper running sessions. This may be because the layouts tend to be exhibited and club nights are needed for repairs, but it may also be because modern exhibition layouts are often not designed for operation. Some of them are not even very much fun to operate – they are designed to be pretty first, to act as a catwalk for rolling stock second, and for operation often only a distant third. This is great for the viewing public but how do the operators feel?

Over the years there have been a few attempts to produce what I would call a 'system' railway: a model railway layout in which several stations are operated by different operators who communicate (in principle) as signalmen would on the real railway, and in which the hidden storage sidings and fiddle-yards so beloved of modellers are (in theory at least!) completely absent. Modellers with large gardens have also created wonderful scenes in which scale-length express trains can run at speed over viaducts and through stations to their driver's content.

However, I suspect that few modern layouts really fulfil the requirements of the system layout properly, and so to redress the balance a little, some of the layouts in this chapter are designed for challenging and fulfilling operation by more than one person. They all involve scenic compromises such as having the termini a few feet apart instead of a hundred miles, but they are all based closely on real railways and can be so operated.

To show what the system layout is all about, consider the old Somerset & Dorset Joint Railway. Was there ever a more fascinating and unusual main line railway? Many people have longed to capture the essence of this line in a model but the problem is always that a single bit of the line rarely portrays the character of the S&D fully because it was the *working* of the line which was special, not just the scenery.

The usual way to design a layout based on a favourite line such as the S&D would be to pick a section of line that looks pretty and bend it around the room, with some storage loops around the back to hold the stock. Plan 8.1 shows the idea, based on the section between Shepton Mallet and Masbury tunnels. As the many viaducts of the S&D are so memorable, it is nice to be able to include two of them, the Bath Road and Charlton viaducts. To do this I have had to shorten Shepton Mallet station significantly and in an 11ft x 8ft room you might prefer to miss out one of the viaducts to portray the station better. However, the curvature of the line fits the room quite well with only a little exaggeration and the result is quite pleasing to the eye, which (to me at least) quite justifies the alterations. The plan could be expanded and straightened a little to suit a club layout and would certainly keep several people busy building it.

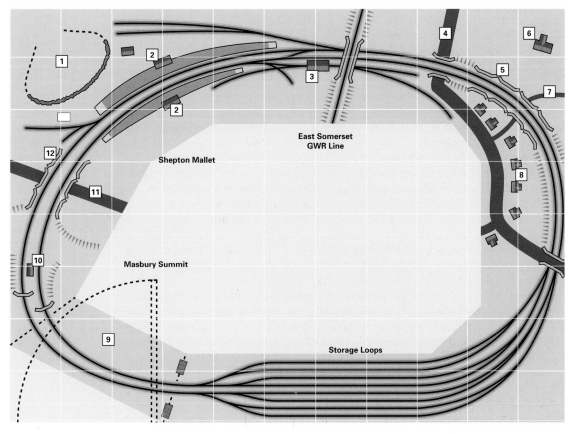

Plan 8.1

Shepton Mallet

1 Stone quarry
2 Station building
3 Goods shed
4 Road
5 Charlton viaduct
6 Farm
7 Lane
8 Town (flat land)
9 Hinged bridge
10 Signalbox
11 Bath Road
12 Bath Road
   viaduct

East Somerset
GWR Line

Shepton Mallet

Masbury Summit

Storage Loops

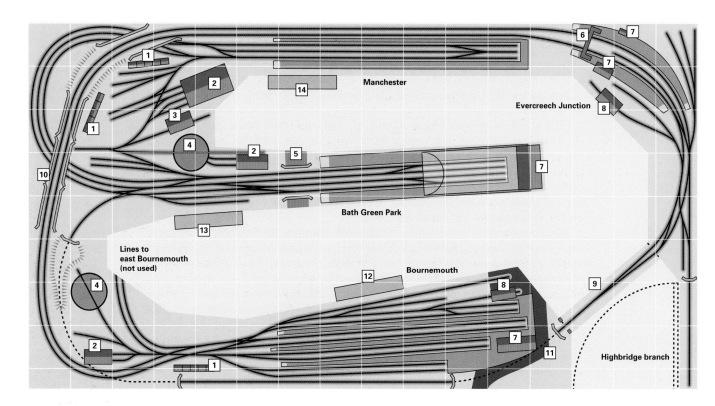

Manchester

Evercreech Junction

Bath Green Park

Lines to
east Bournemouth
(not used)

Bournemouth

Highbridge branch

Plan 8.2

S&D System

1 Terraced houses
2 Engine shed
3 Coal stage
4 Turntable
5 River
6 Footbridge
7 Station
   buildings
8 Goods shed
9 Hinged bridge
10 Viaduct
11 Road
12 Control panel for
    Bournemouth
    operator
13 Control panel for
    Bath Green Park
    operator
14 Control panel
    for Manchester
    operator

What it would *not* do, however, is to keep this band of people interested for very long while operating it. It is very much a layout to be built as an exercise in scenic modelling and then to sit and watch trains go by. Or even to watch them go by while you are painting and assembling the scenery which is what I used to do, and is a pleasant way of spending an evening. But what if your friends want to enjoy operating a model railway rather than just building it and then getting bored? I suggest the answer is to go back to basics and to ask what it is we are trying to do with a model railway. Are we content to create a static scenic model as an outlet for our artistic side, or do we want also to have some fun playing trains?

If the latter is the case then have a look at plan 8.2 which was inspired by the layout that used to be present in the cellars at my old school some forty years ago, though it is quite different in its layout. It is intended to fit a single garage of 16ft length and 8ft 6in width, on the assumption that any band of people sufficiently motivated to build a layout of this complexity will be able to find a garage between them.

Now I admit it is not possible to build truly accurate models of each of the stations on the line in a single garage – a scale model of Bath Green Park alone would take at least two garages end to end, as the Taunton club's superb model showed. But with some moderate compression it is possible to make an easily recognisable model of Bath, Bournemouth, and Evercreech stations and to include enough main line to get the trains running at speed.

All three S&D stations modelled have their correct number of platforms and something close to the real track plan, on the main lines at least. The freight facilities have been cut back severely but the main interest on the layout will probably be in the intensive passenger operation of summer Saturdays. Platforms at Bournemouth can be used for stock storage so there is no need for off-scene storage. The layout is designed to be operable in a prototypical manner by three people but there would be plenty enough activity in the main loco sheds to keep another two busy as well. It also provides an excuse to run the fabulous '9F' locomotives on passenger trains which is well worth building a layout for in my opinion!

The central siding between the running lines at Evercreech Junction holds banking engines such as the S&DJR '7F' and LMS '2P' ready to assist northbound trains over Masbury summit. Heavy trains would be assisted in both directions. The layout would suit Digital Command Control very well but if you use conventional control the Bath controller will need to be a high-power one – trains through Combe Down tunnel would frequently be double-headed and banked at the rear as well, and modelling this could certainly be part of the fun of operation.

Clearly the long-distance trains on summer Saturdays would need somewhere to go from Bath and so I have included a further station for this purpose. It is a very sorry apology for the likes of Manchester Piccadilly or Birmingham New Street and is really little more than a fiddle-yard. But adding some platforms and buildings at least gives the operator reason to do the job properly, and I assume the S&D enthusiast will be much less concerned about accuracy in this LMS station.

There is just room for a recognisable model of the Bath MPD with both the Midland and S&D sheds (the Midland one is the smaller) though as usual the turntable spoils the effect slightly as it can't be compressed. I have run the 'works' line into the other terminus to save adding another turntable there – the entire shed will probably be run by the 'Manchester' operator anyway as the Bath operator will be too busy. Alternatively you can put a turntable on the end of the platform lines as was done in a few places.

It is possible to reduce the plan to fit a smaller space but the platforms at both termini become rather short, so instead I started again and plan 8.3 is the result. This fits a lot of model railway into an 11ft x 8ft room but is a complex layout to build and is not to be recommended for a first layout! However, I have included it here to show some of the techniques used.

Plan 8.3
S&D System compressed

1	Backscene
2	Turntable
3	Coal
4	Engine shed
5	Terraced houses
6	Road
7	Station building
8	Goods shed
9	Footbridge
10	River
11	Viaduct
12	Hinged bridge

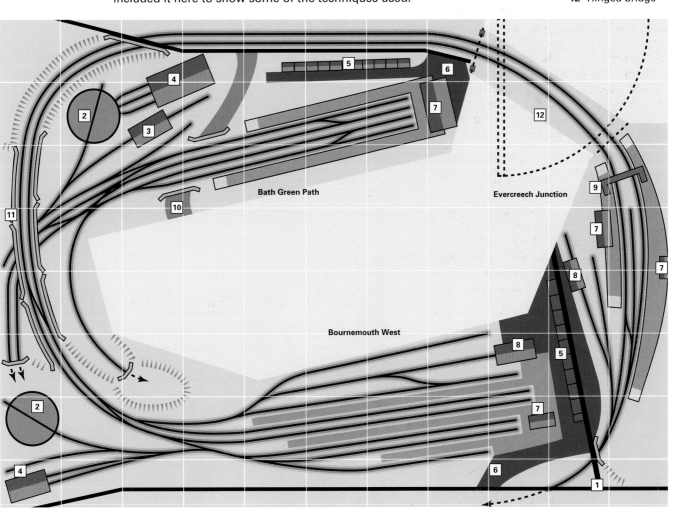

Bath Green Path

Evercreech Junction

Bournemouth West

Although I often avoid using hidden storage loops on system layouts because they usurp the operation that people should be doing, here I have added one because the northbound end of the journey isn't important and there really isn't room for a proper station. The main lines are built on a continuously rising gradient which not only raises Bournemouth station above the low-level storage loops and reverse loop provided for northbound trains out of Bath, but allows a large viaduct to be modelled. This shouldn't really be so close to Bath station but there were plenty of viaducts on the S&D and I feel it helps the atmosphere to include one.

The next thing to notice is the plentiful use of false backscenes. Along the edge of the layout these are used to hide tracks that shouldn't be there, while allowing easy access to them for cleaning and crash removals. But I have also used one across the layout to separate Evercreech Junction from Bournemouth. This backscene doesn't have to be a very tall one with clouds and sky painted on it – a low one with low-relief buildings one side and grass or a roadway the other can also work.

Study the low-level tracks carefully (plan 8.3a); the single-track S&D line from Bath rises at 1 in 48 to clear the storage loops, while the double-track LMS line to the storage loops also drops for the same reason. But the gradient on this line is less and the last bit of each loop is flat to help the trains stop!

You will also notice that all the points on the storage loops are accessible, either behind the backscene or right at the front of the low-level baseboard. If the central part of the low-level baseboard is cut away it is also possible to stick

Plan 8.3a

**Lower level tracks
under Bournemouth**

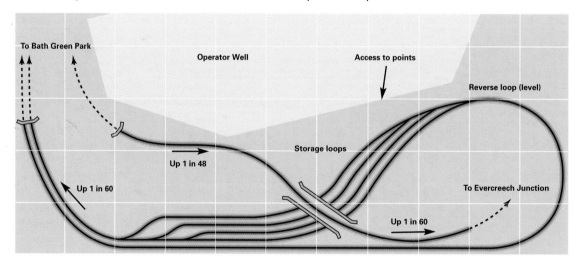

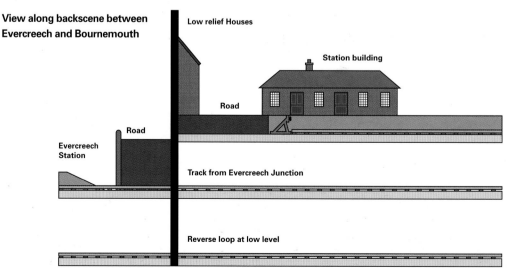

a head and hand up to see the rearmost tracks. Note that none of the 'hidden' tracks are fully out of view for more than about half a train length, so it should be possible to see when a problem has occurred without needing complex electronic indicators.

Bournemouth station is probably the least badly compromised station on this plan, though the loco depot has been brought closer to the station than it should be, and the same is true for Bath. Still in operational terms the layout works as well as the much larger garage-sized layout of plan 8.2 even though the scenery is more heavily compressed, and I rather think I prefer it.

Weymouth

Another prototype with lasting appeal is the Weymouth harbour tramway which ran along the harbour wall from the Town station to the Pier station; this is another line which, due to its length and shape, is very hard to model accurately in the usual way. Once again one could pick a small section of the scene – a vignette, if you like – and model this accurately but I suggest the result would lack the interest of the original, which to my way of thinking relies on the way the line winds itself around the obstacles in its path.

Summer Saturdays in the 1950s and 1960s were always a busy time, with passenger trains filling the Pier station ready for the cross-channel ferries, and seeing these run between cars and houses behind a man with a red flag was a unique spectacle. To capture this atmosphere effectively it is necessary to distort

Plan 8.4

Weymouth

1 Light
2 Pier
3 Dockside wall
4 Cranes
5 Ships
6 Sailing ship
7 Cargo stage
8 Pleasure Palace
9 Terraced
   housing
10 Nothe
   backscene
11 Hill
12 Backscene

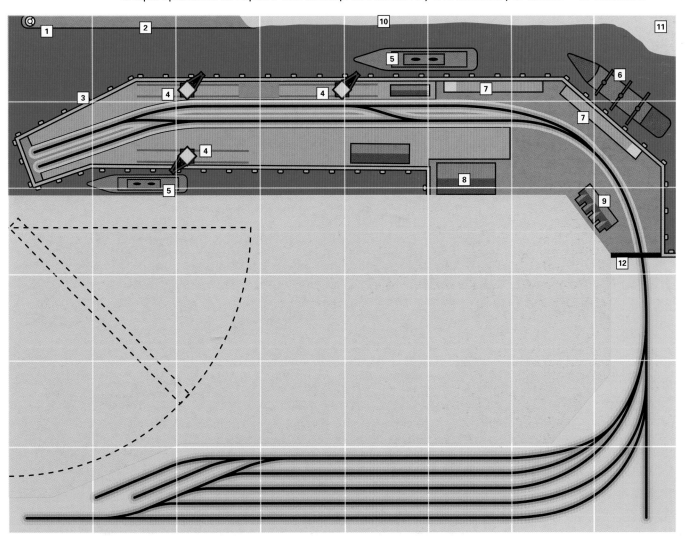

the image, in the same way that a stage painter distorts the geometry of a building to capture its effect. For example the line, although short in railway terms, is actually quite long for a model, which means that it is difficult to fit all of it in a room and still leave somewhere for the trains to go afterwards. On the other hand the line is naturally curved – very sharply, in fact, so it is unusually well suited to being curved around a small room, except that the line naturally faces outwards rather than inwards, so if it goes around the walls of a small room you don't get as good a view as you would hope for.

Still, if you restrict yourself to the Pier station alone a fairly reasonable model is possible in a very small space as plan 8.4 shows. The plan will just fit in the kind of 6ft x 8ft third bedroom found in many modern houses, and it is possible to show part of the harbour and the large grassy hill behind it known as the Nothe. The layout is unashamedly a shunting layout with trains disappearing behind a tall terrace of houses into the fiddle-yard.

Now if you move house or throw the kids out of the nest and find you have a larger room available, then you could re-arrange the same baseboards as in plan 8.5. The new scenic section allows more of the harbour to be modelled including the town bridge, and the two loops on the tramway will make shunting more interesting too. For interest's sake I have altered the trackwork at the pier to the post-1960 version. The original 'Nothe' backscene can be removed from behind the Pier station and put alongside the harbour.

Scenically there is now great scope for modelling artistry around the harbour and town. Both plans allow space for ship models alongside the Pier station and postwar there were electric cranes running along the platform on rails, not unlike the ones still at Bristol docks. The line was used intensively in season by van traffic

Key for Plans 8.5 and 8.6

1 Platform
2 Station building (plan 8.6)
3 Dockside wall
4 Large cranes
5 Ships
6 Sailing ship
7 Cargo stage
8 Pleasure Palace
9 Terrace
10 Boat yard and boats
11 Hill
12 Warehouse
13 Public house
14 Town bridge and road
15 Fishing boats
16 Signalbox
17 Jubilee sidings
18 Lifting bridge
19 Fiddle yard
20 Backscene

Plan 8.5

Weymouth tramway

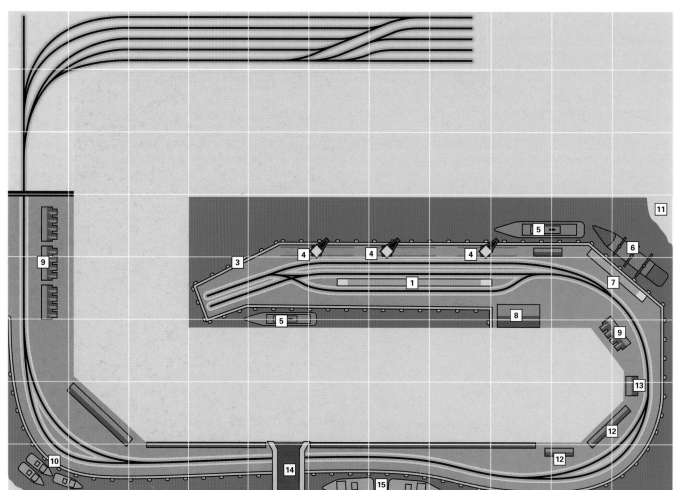

carrying broccoli and tomatoes from the Channel Islands, and photos from the 1950s and 1960s show it crammed absolutely full of vans and shunting engines so you don't have to restrict yourself to passenger trains for realistic operation.

Main Lines

The plans described so far allow railway operation over the tramway but not, strictly, on the main line. Here we come to the main problem with the Weymouth harbour tramway. For most of its life until Bo-Bo diesels came along in the 1960s, the extreme curvature of the line meant it never permitted express engines on its metals – they were all taken off at the Town station and replaced by shunting locomotives. Due to the sharp curves the coaches were even uncoupled and special longer couplings added on each train, though this won't be a problem for our models.

But this does mean that after all the effort of building a layout you can never operate any of your main line locomotives on your layout which is not ideal if (like me) you have accumulated a lot of them! If you want to run these as well then you will need to model the Town station as well, and plan 8.6 shows one way of doing this. Here the room is slightly larger again and the fiddle-yard has been pushed yet further around the room to make way for the Town station and allow the station end of the tramway to be operated prototypically.

Now Weymouth Town station at its peak was a very large station and the track plan has been compressed heavily to fit in a 9ft x 12ft room. To be honest the result is still a little cramped and could be opened out nicely if a garage is

Plan 8.6
**Weymouth
extended tramway**

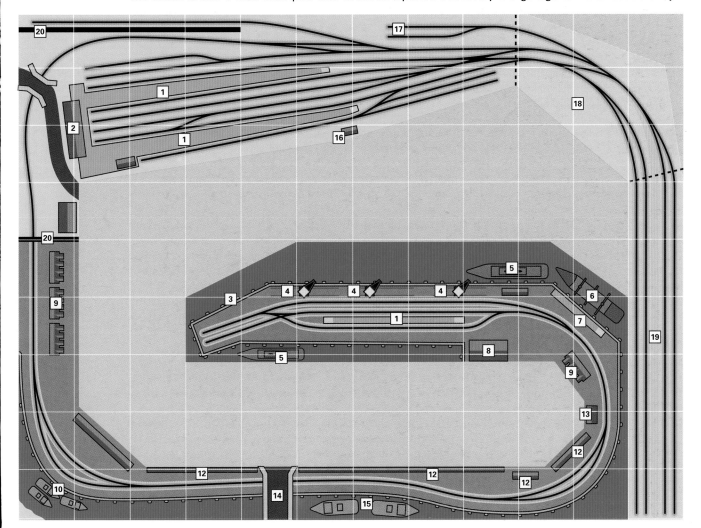

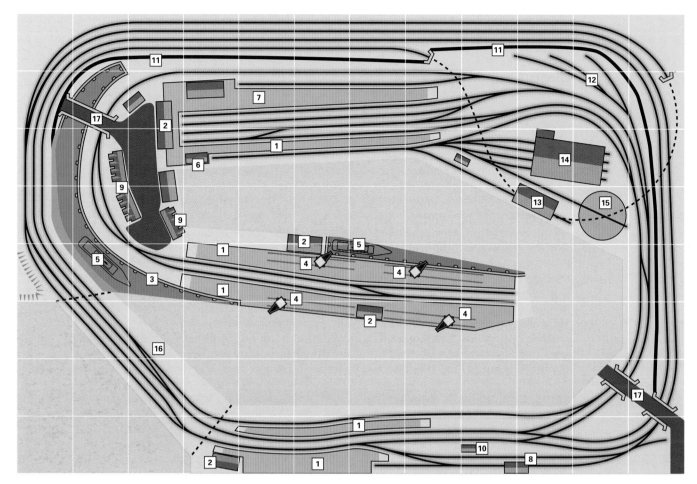

Plan 8.7

**Weymouth
system layout**

1   Platform
2   Station building
3   Dockside wall
4   Large cranes
5   Ships
6   Offices
7   Parcels
8   Goods shed
9   Terrace
10 Signalbox
11 Backscene
12 Jubilee sidings
13 Coal stage
14 Engine shed
15 Turntable
16 Lifting bridge
17 Road

available. But as the station was the effective terminus for many long-distance trains it is worthwhile modelling even in the space shown – photos show both *Flying Scotsman* and *Sir Nigel Gresley* there in the 1960s in addition to the usual SR and GWR express locomotives.

A short spur to a hidden siding represents the Portland branch and would be run with a DMU or auto-coach. Some of the sidings at the station have been included but those familiar with the station will note the loco depot is missing. This is not simply due to lack of space but because of the way the fiddle-yard needs to operate. A main line train which leaves the station enters the fiddle-yard and the locomotive runs to an isolating section at the end of the siding and stops, preferably over a long uncoupling ramp. How do we get a new engine on the other end without hand-shunting?

Simple. A locomotive that has previously arrived at the station departs for the loco depot which is also off-scene, and in reality backs onto the train waiting in the fiddle-yard. At some later time, when the train has left the fiddle-yard and arrived at the station, the locomotive can be released from the isolating section. It leaves the unseen 'loco depot' and backs out to the station. So you can see that adding a proper engine shed and turntable at the station makes this sleight-of-hand impossible unless another turntable is put on the fiddle-yard, which needs more space again and somebody to operate it.

Plans 8.4 to 8.6 were deliberately arranged to show how a layout can develop over time and adapt itself to new locations or to changes in your own ideas. If you find a house move reduces the space available you could even reverse the order of these and avoid breaking up your layout. However, they offer little scope for proper main line running, so in plan 8.7 the whole emphasis of the layout has been changed. The tramway itself has been reduced in importance and is now little more than a spur from the station but the previous fiddle-yard has been replaced with a main line instead. Weymouth Town is included as before, this time with its loco depot, and also a fairly accurate portrayal of Castle Cary station where the Weymouth line met the GWR main line from Paddington.

This allows GWR express trains to run at full speed along the continuous run in addition to diverting Weymouth-bound excursions. There is a low-level reversing loop which is situated underneath the Weymouth Town shed, and this allows trains to return to Weymouth without manhandling. No storage loops per se are provided as the hidden tracks (including the reverse loop) will comfortably hold eight trains, and as each train gets re-formed at Weymouth this should be plenty. The continuous run would suit automation to allow trains to follow one another through the hidden sections but a series of manual section switches will do the job too. The layout is operable with just one person but could occupy two or three when needed as a proper 'system' layout.

Despite its small size Castle Cary station saw plenty of freight action; in addition to pick-up goods, many up freights were banked westwards from the station and the occasional through freight would stop here for a hot-box wagon to be shunted out. In steam days most wagons and vans used grease-filled axleboxes which ran hot on long fast trips and could catch fire if not removed from the train. It was arguably the wholesale replacement of these by oil-filled axleboxes in the 1960s that permitted the removal of the local signalboxes in favour of remote electric boxes, so if you are modelling in steam days this kind of operation can be a nice touch.

There is just room to fit the typical GWR coal stage at Weymouth Town but not the loco coal sidings next to it, so if desired coal trucks could be shunted to and from the Jubilee sidings on the up side instead. Although most of the goods platforms have been lost, the traffic can be dealt with on the short up and down platforms at each side. The middle sidings between the main platforms were used as carriage sidings in those far-off days when trains were lengthened according to need.

Historical Changes and Sources of Information

The S&DJR has almost completely disappeared now but its history is well covered by various books and in extensive photographs and videos by the well-known Ivo Peters. I have studied many of these but there are too many such titles to list individually. For the modeller who needs to build structures most of these books are disappointing as they can each supply only one or two useful pictures. The first three titles listed in the Bibliography are more useful with Ordnance Survey track diagrams but be aware that most of these diagrams date from around 1900; significant track changes occurred by the postwar dates that interest most of us today (this is also true of the otherwise excellent OPC historical guides included in the Bibliography). For example the turntable at Bath Green Park was moved in 1935 and it is difficult to find published pictures of the new one. The R. A. Cooke diagrams (*Track Layout Diagrams GWR Section 18, S&DR*) always give a good indication of which tracks were added and removed at which dates but are unscaled and give no scenic information.

One of the nice things about modelling the Weymouth harbour tramway is that most of the railway is still there. Although trains no longer reach Weymouth Pier on a regular basis, the tracks are still in place and the buildings have hardly changed, so there's no excuse for missing the opportunity to travel there and take pictures. There's even a beach nearby for the kids to play on!

Another important point is that the line is very well covered in photos and books, and although there are many available, I would strongly recommend both *The Weymouth Harbour Tramway* and *The Story of the Westbury to Weymouth Line*. The former is a complete record of the harbour line and pier and includes both history and many extremely useful photos. It also has accurate track plans and photos of all the changes up to the present day which is quite rare. The latter covers the Town station and most of the other stations as far as Westbury in detail with both scaled track plans and signalbox diagrams, and some timetable information and eyewitness accounts too. If only all reference books were so well done as these two! The stations are mostly well preserved, so a visit for photographic purposes is worthwhile.

The Pier station changed several times over its life and the diagrams (plan 8.8a-c) show the main alterations with dates. For most of its life the Pier station had only two tracks until it was rebuilt in 1960 by adding a third track and a very narrow platform shown in the additional sketch, and was rebuilt again in 1973 for the Ro-Ro ferry.

Plan 8.8

Weymouth Pier layout

(not to scale)

1931 – 1960

1   Cargo stage
2   Pleasure Palace
3   Station building
4   Steam cranes
    pre-war
    (electric post-war)
5   Platforms

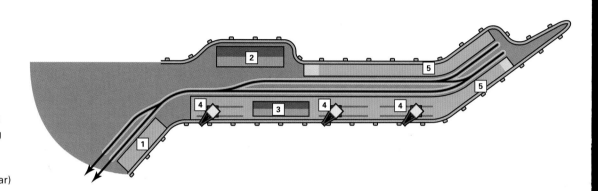

1960 – 1973

1   Cargo stage
2   Pleasure Palace
3   Station building
4   Electric cranes
5   Platforms
6   Movable
    diamond
    and single slip

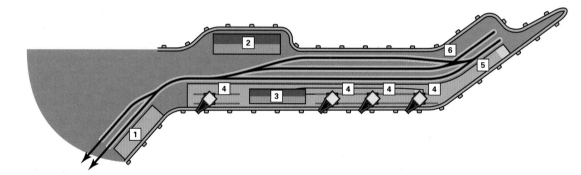

1973 – present

1   Cargo stage
2   Pleasure Palace
3   Station building
4   Roll-on, roll-off
    ferry platform
5   Platforms
6   Large car park

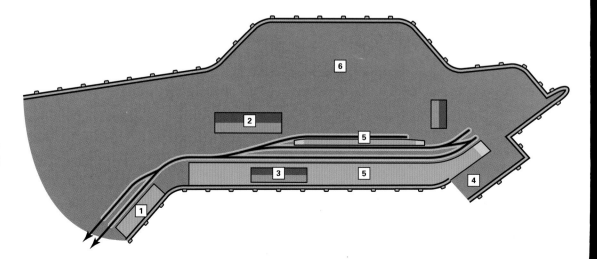

The Weymouth tramway itself has changed little since the end of steam, but the Town station is now but a mere shadow of its former glory with one platform, two faces, and a single-track line leaving the town. In 1950 the Great Western routes south of Dorchester were transferred to the Southern Region and Weymouth became its responsibility, but this didn't have a very great impact on the services and it is important to remember that LSWR and SR trains used Weymouth Town station throughout GWR ownership.

Bournemouth to Weymouth by Mitchell and Smith has some lovely pictures of the Town station in its heyday, including one of the overall roof which was removed in 1951, and the station building which was roughly similar in shape to the old Airfix booking hall. During summer holidays in the 1950s the station was very busy and so two new platform faces were added in 1957. The loco depot lasted until the end of steam (1967) and was removed some time afterwards, many of the sidings going out of use at about the same time. The station itself survived until the new (very much smaller) one was built on the eastern side of the old one in 1987 and the remaining platforms and tracks removed soon afterwards. Their place is now taken by a warehouse and car park.

The Portland branch was lifted in 1970, regular services having stopped many years previously, and little of it remains today. *Bournemouth to Weymouth* also has pictures of the other tramway in this part of the world at Poole harbour, though this never carried passengers and was closed in 1961.

Castle Cary station has hardly altered today, with even the original goods shed and most of the sidings still present. The most obvious change from the track diagram published in *The Story of the Westbury to Weymouth Line* is the removal of the lead into the main line next to the roadbridge and the addition of a platform face for the 'Weymouth' line on the island platform.

For those with broadband internet access the website http://maps.google.co.uk/maps is well worth exploring. If you enter 'Weymouth' in the search box and click on 'satellite' you can zoom in to a satellite picture of Weymouth at a resolution good enough to make out individual sleepers of the track. You are limited to what the picture looked like a year or so ago when the images were recorded but you can follow the tracks around the whole country if you have the time and inclination, and even dismantled lines can often be traced. With the scale that appears on the map you can also measure the dimensions of extant tracks and buildings without any need to hack through undergrowth with a tape measure!

Another website well worth checking is Subterranea Britannica (http://www.subbrit.org.uk) which contains lots of photos of many closed stations, especially (though not exclusively) those near or in tunnels. This has, for example, excellent pictures of the Isle of Wight railways referred to in Chapter 1.

Bibliography

The Somerset & Dorset Then and Now, Hawkins, Mac; Grange, ISBN 1-84013-321-X

Bournemouth to Evercreech Junction (Country Railway Routes series),
    Mitchell, V. & Smith, K.; Middleton Press, ISBN 0-906520-46-0

Bath Green Park to Bristol (Country Railway Routes series),
    Mitchell, V. & Smith, K.; Middleton Press, ISBN 1-901706-36-2

Track Layout Diagrams GWR Section 18, S&DR, Cooke, R. A.;
    1980 (spiral bound, no ISBN)

An Historical Survey of the S&DR, Judge, C. W. & Potts, C. R.;
    OPC, ISBN 0-86093-003-3

Signalman's Morning, Vaughan, Adrian; John Murray, ISBN 0-7195-3827-0

The Weymouth Harbour Tramway, Lucking, John; OPC, ISBN 0-86093-304-0

The Story of the Westbury to Weymouth Line, Phillips, Derek;
    OPC, ISBN 0-86093-514-0

Bournemouth to Weymouth (South Coast Railways series), Mitchell, V. & Smith, K.;
    Middleton Press, ISBN 0-906520-57-6

An Historical Survey of Selected Southern Stations (Vol 1), Pryer, G. A.;
    OPC, ISBN 0-86093-016-5 (Hawkhurst)

An Historical Survey of Selected LMS Stations (Vol 2), Hendry, R. Preston & Hendry,
    R. Powell; OPC, ISBN 0-86903-330-X

An Historical Survey of Selected GW Stations (Vol 1), Clark, R. H.; OPC, ISBN
    0-902888-29-3. (Blagdon, Hemyock, Culmstock and others). See also Vols 2-4.

Great Western Branch Line Termini (Vol 1), Karau, Paul; OPC, ISBN 0-902888-89-7
    See also Vol 2.

An Historical Survey of Great Western Engine Sheds 1947, Lyons, E.;
    OPC, ISBN 0-902888-16-1

Great Western Engine Sheds 1837-1947, Lyons, E. & Mountford, E.;
    OPC, ISBN 0-86093-019-X

Britain's Railways From the Air, Then and Now; Aerofilms, Ian Allan, ISBN
    0-7110-2595-9 (Leeds, Glasgow St Enoch, Weymouth, St Ives and Mallaig)

The Aerofilms Book of Britain's Railways From the Air, Leigh, Chris; Ian Allan,
    ISBN 0-7110-1702-6 (Bembridge, Ramsgate, York, King's Cross, Padstow, Yatton,
    St Ives and Mallaig again)

From the Footplate: Elizabethan, Austin, Stephen; Ian Allan, ISBN 0-7110-2152-X
    (Edinburgh) See also Stephen Austin's other books in the series on named trains,
    with some track diagrams.

Steam Days, January 2008 issue, Red Gauntlet Publications (A long article on
    Leeds Central and its associated yards with lots of useful pictures.)

Hornby Magazine, December 2007 ('Bay Street Shed' and 'Engine Shed Road'
    layouts, both with coaling stages; and 'Railway Realism: Turntables'
    by Alan Earnshaw with lots of turntable photos.)

Subterranea Britannica website at http://www.disused-stations.org.uk

Google Maps website at http://maps.google.co.uk/maps which covers the UK in detail
    but present-day only.

The invaluable Google search engine can help one find an amazing amount of
    information and the various webrings of dedicated modelling and study groups on
    the net (such as the S&DJR Webring site at http://pubs.sdrt.org), all of which are
    worth checking for relevant information and further booklists.

These are, I'm afraid, only a small sample of the many books that have been
    published on these subjects but are the ones I use most frequently for reference
    purposes. There are many other series of books dealing with specific branch lines
    which I cannot list for reasons of space. Although these books go irregularly in
    and out of print, most are available second-hand either from specialist booksellers
    or via the internet. If you need to find any by an internet search, try leaving out the
    dashes and X's in the ISBN number. If you don't have an internet connection you
    can access the web at public libraries and print out relevant details.

Postscript:

The Seven Perils of Layout Design

Railway modelling is without doubt a truly excellent hobby which provides endless hours of harmless amusement without the need for any kind of ball or specialist footwear. However, I have observed that the railway modeller's spouse does not always share enthusiasm for this enterprise and all too often seems to regard the hobby as some kind of sinister disease which prevents the sufferer from completing far more important and rewarding tasks like mowing the lawn, repairing the clock and gluing the picture-frame back together.

Although the true modeller will rightly dismiss this interpretation, after some reflection I have wondered if there might in fact be some small amount of truth in the accusation. My suspicions in this direction were recently confirmed when, while wandering around an old bookshop in Malmesbury, I came across a tattered manuscript which appeared to have escaped from a 17th century medical treatise. After translation from the original Latin and discarding the pages on warts and ague, I was fascinated to see that the accusation is not a recent one at all. Consequently I think the contents are worth sharing for their remarkable insight.

However experienced and worldly-wise we may be, most of us have at some time succumbed to at least one of the Seven Great Perils of Layout Design, and the more prolific of us have tried all seven, though not necessarily in the order given and not generally all at once. These are:

1. **Ovalitis**. The desire to watch express trains running at full speed in an area grotesquely inadequate for the purpose, which results in unseemly tail-chasing around a baseboard which is too obviously made from a flat piece of board. Attempts to disguise this often fall prey to a related condition known as **Rabbitwarrenitis**, in which trains continually run into and out of an excessive number of deeply unconvincing tunnels cut in a hillside of which only a Swiss cheese-lover could be proud, or **Tri-angulation**, an infection sustained by excessive contact with operating accessories of a frivolous nature. Sufferers from this malady can easily be recognised by their layout's inclusion of flying mailbags, helicopters, rockets or spacecraft, plus rolling logs, ducking giraffes and hopper wagons depositing imitation coal at intervals along the track. Chronic over-exposure can also produce allergic reactions to flashing lights, smoke and simulated train sounds. Fortunately these layouts are usually built for children of juvenile and unsophisticated taste by fathers also of juvenile and unsophisticated taste, and can give improbable amounts of pleasure to each.

2. **Freezeritis**. A condition brought about by a release from the confines of (1), often in mature years when a large railway room becomes available, in which the sufferer attempts to fit as much track and as many trains as possible in the space available. Planning such layouts can become an enjoyable monomania but the actuality is often sadly unconvincing, as King's Cross and Crewe overlap along the south wall leaving little room for Edinburgh, Penzance and Ashburton along the other three. However, these layouts are often great fun to operate when one is inebriated and sufficiently far from one's more critical friends to be able to let one's remaining hair down. This condition long pre-dates its discovery and labelling: consequently many of these layouts have survived in suburban attics and spare bedrooms for an astonishingly long time and have therefore become 'classics', to be talked about in hushed tones. Anyone who can drop the correct names and builders of more than three such early examples into a conversation is well on the way to becoming an expert in historical railway modelling.

3. **Branchterminism**. A severe reaction to the above conditions, which seeks to banish all toy-like behaviour and to model instead a simple piece of real railway history, accurately and in as much detail as humanly possible, without regard to time, effort, cost or indeed interest. Such layouts (fortunately no longer *exclusively* modelled on Ashburton GWR) are however excellent apprentice-pieces, and are seen regularly at exhibitions with 'for sale' notices on them. A related condition is:

4. **Fiddleyarditis**, in which the greatest activity on the layout is found in the fiddle-yard, a fascinatingly intricate piece of trackwork completely devoid of scenery. Since this item is often particularly challenging to operate and usually hidden from casual view, the extended absence of trains on the visible section frequently forces younger and less patient visitors to amuse themselves by counting the miniature wildlife artfully scattered along the scenic sections. In extreme cases it has been known for the hidden fiddle-yard to contain about 98% of the rolling stock and pointwork on the layout, but of course the 2% on show is really *very* good. Over time the disease tends to morph into:

5. **Expertosis**, a disease characterised by over-exposure to finescale discussion forums and excessive background research. Carriers of this disease can be recognised by their uncanny ability to spot any historical inaccuracy, however minor, within seconds of arriving at a layout, and by their predilection for sharing this information with everyone else. Contact with carriers of this disease is unwise as it can produce a range of undesirable psychological reactions ranging from mild irritation to severe palpitations. The recommended treatment for suspected infections is to request, politely but firmly, that the sufferer actually display his own scratch-built model of the prototype (or indeed any prototype) for inspection and comparison before any further discussion. This ruse is particularly effective when the sufferer is also infected (as is commonly the case) by:

6. **Completaphobia**. A severe condition affecting many mature modellers in which sustained examination of modelling requirements and extensive consideration of the ultimate design which meets all the previously determined modelling requirements leads to a state of mental stress in which no definite decision can be made without being rescinded or amended the following week. Sufferers are condemned always to tear up a layout just before completion (but usually just after the most complex trackwork has been laid) as they have suddenly realised a much better way of doing it. In extreme cases the condition further evolves into:

7. **Armchairitis**, in which the planning and re-planning occurs in such a repetitive and vicious cycle that no building work on the layout actually occurs at all. The chronic sufferer of this debilitating malaise can expect to create enormous piles of paper with unintelligible and usually unlabelled sketches on them but cannot, alas, find time even to clean the dust off the unfinished layout let alone complete it. The layout is likely to end up serving as a complex 3-dimensional shelf for tools, battery chargers, pots of glue and paint, pairs of glasses, rubber gloves, broken locomotives that just need a *small* repair to run again, and almost everything else that apparently doesn't have any other place to go. On the other hand the sufferer is well placed to write books describing how other people can design and build a layout.'